STRONG WORDS FOR THE WEEK

by Sherod "Sha Stimuli" Khaalis

RoseDog Books

PITTSBURGH, PENNSYLVANIA 15238

RoseDog Books
585 Alpha Drive
Suite 103
Pittsburgh, PA 15238
Visit our website at www.rosedogbookstore.com

ISBN: 978-1-64957-980-5
eISBN: 978-1-63661-055-9

Edited by Bryan Kayser
Front cover designed by Big Drew Grafix

FOREWORD

My name is Sherod Khaalis Williams. Ever since I was a young adolescent, I had the dream to become a star as a hip-hop recording artist. My older brother Lord Digga allowed me to tag along to studio sessions when I was a teen while he was crafting music for himself, Masta Ace, and the Notorious B.I.G. As an adult, I created a persona and a character named **Sha Stimuli**, and he existed as the brazen, egotistical, more assertive version of myself.

After graduating from Delaware State University, I made my childhood dream a reality and signed with a major record label, Virgin Records. That was back in 2005, the same year that I bumped into my future wife at our ten-year high school reunion. In between then and now, I've experienced an extreme transition from a young rapper with a self-absorbed mission to a grown man raising a family.

I endured intense spiritual growth and what I would consider some of the most arduous years of my adulthood. I didn't realize how dark my days had become until enlightenment was bursting through the scars and scabs on my soul. The writings you are about to sit with are part of the reason I made it through. For one year, I decided to write a verse every week. I got halfway through the year and then I stopped. And for the rest of the year, I read one of those verses every week. I used my rhythmic writings as tools to vent and learn about myself simultaneously. I noticed how my verses evolved and shifted from artful expression to hopeful inspiration that might actually assist others. I have compiled some of those pieces and added additional guidance from my last few trips around the sun. I included breakdowns and anecdotes explaining the intention behind the bars, and an action item for you at the end of each verse and annotation. I want to thank you for taking this journey and I hope that every week you can find something to focus on that will motivate you to be greater than the day before.

Sherod Khaalis

TABLE OF CONTENTS

WEEK 1

THE CHILLS

Being broke at 30, it can give you the chills,
When Biggie said that, I was little, thinking, "30 is ill!
I will be rich when I get old, and I'm achieving all my goals!"
But I was 29 and crying, I had just lost my deal,
I was sulking, feeling helplessness,
Living proof that hell exists,
I had lost my way 'cause I was so consumed with selfishness,
Totally forgot about the times that I accepted gifts,
From family and friends, and my girl gave me an extra lift,
I'm the one that told myself I'm not allowed to try,
I was spitting, "People live each day like you're about to die,"
I made myself a promise,
Now I'm watching Eric Thomas,
Thinking, "Damn, I drifted off, 'cause I forgot about the 'Why,'
Why did I decide to put words on top of instruments?
Why did I spend years of developing selfless discipline?
Why did I desire providing for all my fam?
And then why did my lack of fans make me feel like I'm insignificant?"
How come you get mad because you wake up and it's Monday?
You claim you have a long week ahead of you,
My homie has cancer and her lungs ache,
And sometimes breathing is unbearable,
So she can only wish she has a long week,
Followed by some months, and a year or two,
I'm sorry if this sounds like a harsh speech,
But mostly I am talking to the mirror too,
Wake up

The cover to my 2012 EP entitled *The Chills*. Yes that's a Waffle House shirt; no I never worked there.

THE CHILLS

Being broke at 30, it can give you the chills,
When Biggie said that, I was little, thinking, "30 is ill!
I will be rich when I get old, and I'm achieving all my goals!"
But I was 29 and crying, I had just lost my deal,

The Notorious B.I.G aka Biggie Smalls is my favorite rapper of all time. He had a very popular freestyle verse back in the mid-90s where he spit the phrase:

"Hanging with the ni—as don't pay the bills/And being broke at 30, gives a ni—a the chills..."

When I heard the line, I was a teenager. I had a distinct fear of living those words he rapped about. I don't think he realized what the chills would signify for the listeners of his words. Three decades of life became a benchmark for me. My goal was to be a millionaire, or a famous rapper, or, worst-case scenario, out of my mother's house before I turned 30. My mother was my protector and my idol. She raised my older brother and I while maintaining a house in Flatbush, Brooklyn with one household income. We always had meals, she never missed any utility payments, and she worked at the phone company for over 35 years. I wanted to leave my mom's nest and do more than survive, I wanted to thrive and be successful.

30 years of life was considered old. 30 was the end of your youth. 30 meant that you could no longer "try" to make it at something. You had to be at your destination by 30, or you were a failure in my eyes. That was my logic. I kept that way of thinking for many years, and then one day I woke up and I was 29 years old. I had stumbled into the realm of being an independent artist with a mission to make ends meet and hopefully wander back into the mainstream by some miraculous feat. My income was spotty, my girl was in the south, I was in New York, and most importantly, I had not moved out on my own. My biggest fear had become a reality.

I was sulking, feeling helplessness,
Living proof that hell exists,
I had lost my way 'cause I was so consumed with selfishness,
Totally forgot about the times that I accepted gifts,
From family and friends, and my girl gave me an extra lift,

We've all hit hurdles and felt like the world was ending. Life resembled an apocalypse once I came to the realization that I had managed to lose what I dreamt of my entire life. The record deal was symbolic to me. It was a goal that I had achieved, and it was equivalent to making the NBA or getting a really high-paying job after college. I was a decent basketball player with average athleticism and an inconsistent outside shot. I graduated Cum Laude from Delaware State University with a degree in Mass Communication, but I didn't take the normal route after leaving school. I pretty much chased an elusive goal that seemed impossible at times. I was extremely ecstatic when I realized the impossible became possible. I had finally done something to make my mother proud until I had to face the fact that it was gone.

When I was Sha Stimuli, I solely focused on my own ambitions. Of course I wanted to buy my mom a house and maybe have a child at some point, but my daily agenda was about me. I had a hellacious desire to be famous. I was masquerading as a fictional character that I had created.

It was during those times of indecision and insecurity that I leaned on my future wife mildly. I didn't want her to know how lost I was, but just the hint of misdirection and uncertainty was enough for her to prompt me to move to Atlanta and find other means of income other than rapping for food. After years of us maintaining a long distance relationship, I decided to take the necessary steps to move to Atlanta. Life would get very complex for me as I shuffled back and forth between my mother's home in Brooklyn and my girl's apartment in ATL. I wasn't paying bills at either place, and I was doing whatever I could to make money. This was a rough patch that I endured and now that I can look back at those times, I realize I did not communicate with the two people who were looking out for me the most. I was falling out of love with music and I did not know my next move. My relationships suffered because I feared being honest. It was a life lesson that I learned from.

I'm the one that told myself I'm not allowed to try,
I was spitting, "People live each day like you're about to die,"

"Back in high school, I didn't make the team, I kept trying out/grown man now, I took the word 'trying' out/ of my vocabulary now I'm scared to die without/changing the globe, I'm breaking the mold..."

This line is from my song entitled "The Title" released in 2012.

I had so many insightful lines about pursuing goals, chasing dreams, not being a slave to set salaries, and most importantly, to live like you're dying. What that meant to me was to go hard at your passion until it feeds your lifestyle. The issue with that is my passion wasn't truly identified.

I assumed I had the passion to be a legendary emcee, but it was so much deeper. My soul attempted to fill me in but I wasn't brave enough to listen.

Question: If you know how to make songs without profanity and it gives you a feeling of pride, why not continue to do that?

Answer: Because you're afraid that fans won't respect you being an intellectual college graduate spewing positivity. Music laced with profanity and hints of violence and ignorance can create the right balance for an artist who does not have valid street credibility.

Question: When you want to dress in a style that suits you, and it may not contain flashy jewelry or the typical star costume, what prevents you from going with your gut?

Answer: The people around you convince you that there is a formula to success. It's not their fault. They were doing what someone else taught them.

My misstep was that I was trying to fit in and it didn't feel genuine. I was wearing shiny chains and going to clubs every night to be seen until it felt like a chore. If I was truly living like there was no tomorrow, I would have put out the music I wanted, dressed in a way that made me comfortable, and stayed home on those nights I didn't feel like being out. Do exactly what you feel and let people decide to tune in or change the channel.

I made myself a promise,
Now I'm watching Eric Thomas,
Thinking, "Damn I drifted off, 'cause I forgot about the 'Why,'
Why did I decide to put words on top of instruments?
Why did I spend years of developing selfless discipline?
Why did I desire providing for all my fam?
And then why did my lack of fans make me feel like I'm insignificant?"

Eric Thomas is one of my favorite motivational speakers. I often feel like I am the rhythmic version of a motivational speaker that isn't quite polished at speaking. Eric's stories and his energy have been a consistent force in my life to provoke action steps. With that said, he talks about finding your "why" and using it as fuel when you need it to keep going.

My "why" was easily defined when I was a young college graduate. I liked to rap, I was good at it, and without Biggie around, I felt a void in the music industry that I wanted to fill. As time went on, I got less confident about my ability to gain true fans because of my laid-back personality and unclear image.

I started to become confused about my reason for entering the music industry. For years I wanted to create a lane of music that would feed people's souls with authentic truths, as well as give them vibrations of fun and lighthearted singles.

After a contractual bind that kept me from releasing music for a year, I was grasping for a lifeline that would give me any visibility. I believed I was growing as an artist at one point, but the Internet measures an artist's reach with data. Whether it's the number of listens on a hip-hop website, the amount of followers on social media, or the lack of views on a video, I quickly realized that my fandom was not enough to sustain a luxurious life. People were not responding to my craft and I had to face the hard truth that I was not relevant to a wide audience. I understood that and it was not easy to accept.

How come you get mad because you wake up and it's Monday?
You claim you have a long week ahead of you,
My homie has cancer and her lungs ache,
And sometimes breathing is unbearable,
So she can only wish she has a long week,
Followed by some months, and a year or two,
I'm sorry if this sounds like a harsh speech,
But mostly I am talking to the mirror too,
Wake up

A friend of mine told me that I didn't need a large amount of fans because I had super fans that connected with my stories. He knew one of those super fans personally and he put me on the phone with a young lady named Katherine one day. I always downplayed my notoriety so I was shocked that she knew so much of my music and as she explained her connection to my debut album *My Soul To Keep*, she shed tears. I was speechless and did not understand the impact that my music had on her.

I found out later that she was stricken with cancer and my music was instrumental in her therapeutic process. Katherine became my muse as she embodied my reason for becoming a rapper. I wanted my words to affect lives, and I wanted to know exactly how listeners digested my food for thought. Her bravery and vulnerability was more than admirable, following her journey made me want to be a better human.

After that convo, she got my email address and I would send songs here and there and we had some correspondence. I constantly prayed for her, I sent her some merchandise, and I reached out sometimes to see how her treatments were going, but I didn't reach out enough. We hadn't spoken in years when her mother called me and left a message for me using my real name. I called her mother back, assuming she had the wrong number, but her mom had a lot of info about me. She knew my music, my wife's name, and that I had sons. Then she told me that I knew her daughter and she wanted to inform me that she had passed away. It was a strange conversation, but my heart dropped and I was filled with emotions ranging from despair to guilt.

I wished I could have told Katherine that there were lines inspired by her life. I wish I had sent more merchandise to her, along with more emails to check on her, and any kind thoughts more frequently. I am running down this whole story to say that Katherine always reminds me to be happy on Mondays. Some people want Monday to last as long as possible because they might not see Tuesday. Each day is so precious and hearing about the intense treatment my friend was going through made me appreciative of the small elements that add to my happiness.

· · · · ·

Week 1 To-Do List: Identify the reason or reasons for your passion. If you don't have a passion, figure out the reason for your career choice. If you are not yet working in your career of choice, then there is some position that you can see yourself in, that is the job I want you to focus on and ask yourself why you're interested in the field. Once you have it, write it down and hold onto it. Refer to it when you can or when you need to be reminded.

WEEK 2

THE GREEN LIGHT

I don't know what you're going through,

I don't know what you're going through,

I don't know what you're going through,

But happiness is overdue,

So what your finances are <u>tied up</u>,

Like <u>overtime</u>,

And you overused your overtime,

And you're on the grind,

To get more dough, you gotta go to school,

But to go to school, you need more dough,

And it flows slow, and you're so confused,

You ask, "How do I live? Where do I go? Who do I pray to?

What am I supposed to do?"

You hear shots firing, then cop sirens, then cops firing,

And the force they use,

Could kill your kid, it's so morbid,

You want to forfeit, we're not born to lose,

I don't pretend that I know all the right words to say,

People say, "Follow your dreams, don't give up, keep believing,

let go and let God, pray,"

You say you're around 35

With hurt in your eyes from a job you despise with low pay,

Or maybe you're still in your twenties,

Not making real money, and everyone's sounding cliché,

All I can tell you is I would keep falling,

Asking the Lord for my calling,

He would hang up, I kept calling,

Cursing like, "Why are you stalling?"

Almost felt like I was stalking,
I'm not just talking,
I questioned the path I was walking,
Just nod your head if you do that too often,
Every time I think I'm going through something,
I envision myself in a coffin,
I don't know what you're going through,
If no father figure is close to you,
If you're 17 and you're selling "trees,"
And got enemies, so you're holding tools,
You hear rap songs where they're trap gods,
And they act hard, but you know the rules,
You need to be about, what you rhyme about,
So go try that route and be on the news,
See I've been through the fire,
Sold to the buyers,
Never locked up, I came close and retired,
Face been on fliers, for bars that inspire,
That's why I got hired, to take people higher,
Find your desires, I'm out here trying,
Kids are the future, the youth, they need guidance,
Life is so final, you cannot rewind it,
So live every day like you're dying
Go!

I think I was speaking at my mother's 40th birthday party in Miami, Florida. I was 10 years old and I loved public speaking. That part in my hair though…

THE GREEN LIGHT

I don't know what you're going through,
I don't know what you're going through,
I don't know what you're going through,
But happiness is overdue,

I have no idea what trouble, drama, issue, or obstacle you are facing at the moment. I don't know what you've been through, what you've lost, or what will help you specifically.

I do know that we have all felt as if happiness had to be purposefully pursued. I know that at some point in your life, you felt as though obtaining a certain amount of money, a position, or some type of social status would bring you joy. Most of us believe that we should depend on other humans to make us feel better about ourselves.

This journey is not about fixing a problem or figuring out some deep, twisted riddle that begins and ends with you. It is simply about someone that was lost who decided to share, and your ability to relate it to your own life and apply any action that fits. For now, let's start with happiness.

Years ago, when I was first starting my transition from rapper to educator, I was a substitute teacher. I remember filling in for an English teacher at a school in Sandy Springs, Georgia. On the teacher's desk, she had a toy with a smiley face on it. It was more like a big button that looked like something one would find in a random gift shop. On the front of the yellow smiley face it read, "Want a laugh?" I stared at it the whole first period while the students were in the class. I was so curious to push it and hear a funny joke. I wondered if it would make me laugh. The suspense grew as my first free period was upon me and I had no students for the next 40 minutes. Right away, I closed the door and pushed the button.

Was it broken? There was no joke. The thing just laughed at me. It was a hearty laugh. And for a second, I was truly disappointed. I wanted to laugh; I didn't want "a laugh." And that's when it hit me…I didn't have to wait for a joke to smile. I didn't have to wait for someone to make me happy. I was in a strange and unfamiliar place in life where I felt like a failure, but life was speaking to me and saying that everything would be just fine.

So what your finances are <u>tied up</u>,
Like <u>overtime</u>,
And you overused your overtime,
And you're on the grind,
To get more dough, you gotta go to school,
But to go to school, you need more dough,
And it flows slow, and you're so confused,
You ask, "How do I live? Where do I go? Who do I pray to?
What am I supposed to do?"

In sports when the score is tied up, the game continues in overtime. Similarly, when you have used up your scheduled work-time but you need to score more income, overtime is used. Overtime symbolizes the fact that the time you were allotted for a duty was not enough. Overtime defines grind just as much as going back to school to get more degrees to earn more money. But the cyclical task of spending more, taking out more loans, and learning more just so you can earn more doesn't always seem like a favorable equation for the average person.

I've been in a space where my salary did not measure up to my financial goals and my overall view of my self-worth. But I didn't believe another degree was the answer. My wife, like most people who continue their education, was not focused on a payday from her Masters Degree. She made a wise choice to go back to school because it has paid off for our family. So as I asked some difficult questions to the man in the mirror, the most important one was answering what I really wanted out of life. Did I see myself as a full time writer, counselor, or educator? Was money my honest motivation? My inspiration came from my desire to change lives. Even if my salary was not indicative of my role or my worth, I knew it was temporary.

The best answer to some of the questions that stumped me was, "I don't know." It was refreshing to be honest with myself and say that no matter how many years I had fumbled around the planet, it was perfectly fine to be unsure of my next move. I embraced that.

You hear shots firing, then cop sirens, then cops firing,
And the force they use,
Could kill your kid, it's so morbid,
You want to forfeit, we're not born to lose,

Just when you get into a groove of going inward and improving yourself, being honest with the mirror, and allowing happiness to seep in, the world kicks you in the aorta and footage of another cop killing someone of color reaches the news.

Whether you identify as a person of color or you're simply someone who empathizes, the pain is severe. The idea of human life being devalued over and over is enough to cripple your daily thoughts for moments at a time.

Sometimes as a Black man, my day can shift, and hatred and contempt start to grow unhealthily with no direct target. I am also a father to two African-American boys and I have to decide how I will introduce the idea of police brutality, racism, and classism to them. I want to instill pride in my children. I want them to have pride in their heritage, pride in their nationality, and pride when it comes to being individuals. These crimes, as heinous as they may be, are a reminder that we can always reach out to assist others. The more love we spread, the better the chances that we might alter the next dark, racist heart.

I don't pretend that I know all the right words to say,
People say, "Follow your dreams, don't give up, keep believing, let go and let God,
pray,"
You say you're around 35
With hurt in your eyes from a job you despise with low pay,
Or maybe you're still in your twenties,
Not making real money, and everyone's sounding cliché,

All I can tell you is I would keep falling,
Asking the Lord for my calling,
He would hang up, I kept calling,
Cursing like, "Why are you stalling?"
Almost felt like I was stalking,
I'm not just talking,
I questioned the path I was walking,
Just nod your head if you do that too often,
Every time I think I'm going through something,
I envision myself in a coffin,

The boys that my wife and I are raising are the absolute greatest blessing we could have hoped for. As blessed as we are, we're both in the not-so-young category raising young children and at times it can be challenging. Our oldest boy, Zaire is unable to wipe his own behind while the youngest, Cairo, is in diapers. I have witnessed moments where they are sad because of some factor that they may not understand. Zaire can get sleepy and irritable often. He may even cry for something that my wife and I deem miniscule. But when we are in a mental space that is not moved by anger or impatience, we react with kindness to his crying fits. We listen, we kneel down to his eye level, and we acknowledge that a young child does not have the vocabulary to express their true feelings.

If you're 35 years old, it may not be socially accepted to let out a cry when you can't find the words. At 20-something, it's frowned upon to lie down and wallow in tears simply because your life isn't where you expected it to be. Even though adults have the words, we don't always use them effectively. I rarely have the magical phrases to console my children. Sometimes a hug is all that's needed for them to feel better. As much as I find myself telling Zaire and Cairo to stop crying, I want to teach them to feel comfortable expressing any emotions the same way I speak to The Creator when I am at a crossroad.

Speaking of crossroads, envisioning a coffin and thinking about the afterlife are mental exercises that are not meant to be morbid. Those thoughts are intended to remind me that life is grand. While funerals can be brimming with sorrow and grief, they can also serve as mortality reminders that have the ability to assist us in making every second count. Sometimes, the thought of dying helps me live.

I don't know what you're going through,
If no father figure is close to you,
If you're 17 and you're selling "trees,"
And got enemies, so you're holding tools,
You hear rap songs where they're trap gods,
And they act hard, but you know the rules,
You need to be about what you rhyme about,
So go try that route and be on the news,
See I've been through the fire,
Sold to the buyers,
Never locked up, I came close and retired,
Face been on fliers, for bars that inspire,
That's why I got hired, to take people higher,
Find your desires, I'm out here trying,
Kids are the future, the youth, they need guidance,
Life is so final, you cannot rewind it,
So live every day like you're dying
Go!

I've touched on happiness, finances, external factors, and crossroads. I wanted to address the youth, and the music that I grew up listening to. Music guided me in some instances when a traditional father figure was absent.

I looked to Chuck D and KRS-1 to shed knowledge in the areas I was clueless about. I observed videos and the lifestyles of my favorite artists and learned about the pitfalls of money and violence. I witnessed Eazy-E speak out against law enforcement and then lose his life to a fatal disease. I saw Tupac Shakur get arrested numerous times after achieving fame and stardom, and then ultimately lose his life for what seemed to be a senseless altercation. As a youngster, I was learning what to do and what not to do, and hip-hop was somewhat of an instructor.

Today, I'm not sure what messages are being promoted to our teens. I know that drug usage has expanded to cough medicine mixtures and pills. I know that violence and weaponry are praised and exploited on social media, and I know that the radio stations play music that is flooded with negative concepts that could contribute to the downfall of many of our young brothers and sisters. But that is a skewed view from an old man that is not heavily involved in an industry I was once engulfed in. I was so deep in it, that I tried to dabble in criminal activities with the hopes that I would gain notoriety and credibility for my illegal actions. But today, I want the children of this world to know that even if I cannot produce the music chart-topping song that will lift their spirits, I have substituted that role with one that puts me in the face of many young-sters daily. I am able to pour my own positivity into them, and I am truly grate-ful for that opportunity. Whether you're a youngster ready to change the world, or in the middle of life's quest looking for an alternate path to greatness, live each day with the passion of someone who doesn't know when time will expire. Go!

· · · · ·

Week 2 To-Do List: Write your bucket list. It can be long or short but give some thought to deeds you would like to do, trips you want to take, even include family plans, activities, or luxurious items you want to buy. Put them on paper or in your phone and sit with the list for a moment. Internalize how hard or simple it might be to cross some actions off of your list. Go!

WEEK 3

THE PRESSURE

What do you do when you feel pressure on?
Bills overdue and your check is gone,
And the friends you keep checking on,
They don't check on you, because you're the strong friend,
And what doesn't kill you, will keep you strong,
I had to start screaming at the mirror because we just couldn't get along,
That peaceful part inside me passed away and I've been reborn,
Since God sent me, I had friends that would <u>resent me</u>,
<u>It killed me</u> and then <u>He re-sent me</u>,
I'm more than an emcee,
I feel like I deserve all your offerings
Since my pops had second thoughts and almost turned to abortion,
I guess that's why I love life, and try to learn from my losses,
I hit the streets, and <u>watch my step</u> like <u>fraternities crossing</u>,
I know <u>misery loves company</u>, but if you check your history,
You work for a company, <u>companies love misery</u>,
I don't let things get to me,
Enemies don't exist to me,
Lost my way in the industry,
Losing has led to victory,
Criticize when they mention me,
Wonder what he was meant to be,
Penny Hardaway, Tracy McGrady, without the injuries,
Love - they won't give to me,
But I don't stress it though; it's like a <u>medical test result,</u>
<u>I need negativity!</u>
So when a hater is aggressively passive,
With little questions they're asking,
And sounding skeptic, sarcastic,
Don't let it distract you; I swear it's a blessing attraction,
It can't affect me, it injects me with passion, How do you handle pressure?

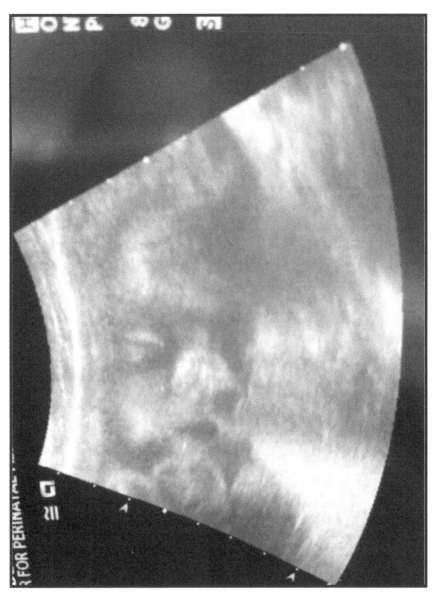

This is the Ultrasound photo of my first son Zaire. I felt intense pressure knowing he was on his way. I stared at this picture often as I wondered what he would look like.

THE PRESSURE

What do you do when you feel pressure on?
Bills overdue and your check is gone,
And the friends you keep checking on,
They don't check on you, because you're the strong friend,
And what doesn't kill you, will keep you strong,

What does pressure mean to you? The type of pressure I'm mentioning here is financial pressure to maintain a residence and the basic essentials needed to stay alive. Some of us hit obstacles once in a while, and we may get behind on bills, or have some late payments, but is that truly pressure? Are finances more of a pressing issue when you have offspring and they don't understand the logistics of income and outcomes?

What if you're the friend that is supposed to pick other people up? Do you ever let anyone know that you may not have your life in order? Pressure can come in the form of a health scare, or it may be when someone close to you isn't doing great. When you feel it, what do you do?

I had to start screaming at the mirror because we just couldn't get along,
That peaceful part inside me passed away and I've been reborn,
Since <u>God sent me</u>, I had friends that would <u>resent me</u>,
<u>It killed me</u> and then <u>He re-sent me</u>,

There comes a time in our lives where we have to face ourselves and be as honest as possible. I was tired of walking on eggshells with myself because I was afraid to admit that my dream had changed. I was keeping the peace within me because recognizing the truth would disrupt my existence. Although I don't believe you can really lose because life is filled with victories and hurdles, and wins and lessons, I had to constantly remind myself of that fact. My lessons felt like losses.

Have you ever been close to someone because of a common interest or situation? Were you only best buddies with someone while you guys were in school, or co-workers, but as soon as that common road closed, you drifted? When you're in entertainment, there are often multiple people that bring their talents together to create a project. Managers, publicists, producers, and anyone else involved, all work diligently to reach a goal. For me that goal was a record deal, at another point in my life it was a series of mixtapes, and then it was an album. I had a tough time dealing with the fact that my friends were only my friends when we were spending time daily trying to advance in the music business. It made me question whether or not I was honest with them and if we were really friends at all.

I'm more than an emcee,
I feel like I deserve all your offerings
Since my pops had second thoughts and almost turned to abortion,
I guess that's why I love life, and try to learn from my losses,
I hit the streets, and watch my step like fraternities crossing,
I know misery loves company, but if you check your history,
You work for a company, companies love misery,

This is not literal, but how many of us work for companies that have owners and CEOs that we don't meet or see everyday? When I say companies love misery, what that means is that when you're young, you tend to have a mission, goal, or objective. When you get set in a position with a salary (unless you're an educator), your role is to fund someone else's mission. Your job is to punch in and run a division of a department of a corporation that was created by someone that generated enough money that they can pay you to not create your own company. So in essence, that CEO doesn't necessarily want you miserable when you work for their company but they don't want you too excited either because you might start to get some ideas floating in your head that you can do whatever you put your mind to.

I used to watch the movie *Up in the Air* quite often. It stars George Clooney (Ryan) as a consultant for firms that needed assistance when firing employees. He reminded me of myself at one time. His life was constantly on the road, he lived out of a suitcase, and none of his relationships were long lasting.

There's a compelling scene where Ryan had to break the news to an executive of a company, Bob (played by J.K. Simmons) that he was being laid off.

Bob was not thrilled at all about the decision and raised his voice. Ryan, who was supposed to be comforting in these moments, became brutally honest. He suggested that Bob's kids were not his biggest fans and then he posed the question:

"Do you know why kids love athletes?
Because they follow their dream."

And after Bob put down his guard a bit, Ryan asked him how much the company, that he gave decades of his life to, offered him in the beginning to give up on his dream. He answered with a modest salary that put things in perspective. Bob wasn't living for himself. The dream he had before he got the job fizzled away. His salary was meant to replace the joy he desired when he imagined his dream career. Companies love misery.

Ultimately, when you walk out of that door, whatever work you do, make sure you are working for your own personal advancement in some way.

I don't let things get to me,
Enemies don't exist to me,
Lost my way in the industry,
Losing has led to victory,
Criticize when they mention me,
Wonder what he was meant to be,
Penny Hardaway, Tracy McGrady, without the injuries,
Love - they won't give to me,
But I don't stress it though; it's like a medical test result,
I need negativity!

Losing led to victory. Think about that for a second. How many times has a loss led to a win for you? I know I have countless stories.

I got cut from the team and then worked my butt off to get ten times better.

I got mediocre grades until I was tired of playing around and I needed to show my potential.

I got dropped from my label, my music career went sour, I left New York, the part time writing gig I had folded as the entire site went down, I moved to Atlanta with my fiancé, we ended up calling off the wedding, and then we broke up and I had to move out on my own, I was a former signed rapper walking into schools as a substitute teacher.

My principal assured me that if I passed some standardized tests he would hire me as a Special Education English teacher. I passed the tests and he gave the job to someone else. I lost, and lost, and lost again.

But it all led me to victory. Victory I couldn't see because at the time, it all felt like multiple disappointments. Once I became focused on the lessons, I was embracing every stage, every second of agony. How can I have an enemy? How can I wonder about what would've been? I'm here. It's about today. And I have to admit that sometimes when I get that "no," or refusal, or someone turns down a script, or says a book idea won't work, I get enthusiastic. I know the energy of my intentions is filled with integrity so the goals I've set are going to happen.

So when a hater is aggressively passive,
With little questions they're asking,
And sounding skeptic, sarcastic,
Don't let it distract you; I swear it's a blessing attraction,
It can't affect me; it injects me with passion,
How do you handle pressure?

I remember when I first got to Delaware State University. I was overwhelmed with the sea of Black faces at the prestigious HBCU. I had just come from a junior college playing basketball in Iowa for one year and I wasn't sure how I would handle the transition going from a small school in the middle of no-where to a school with a totally different demographic and gender ratio. I planned on getting a 4.0 the first semester just to set a standard for myself.

When I voiced my academic mission to my new friends, two of them chuckled as if that was impossible. I wasn't a highly intelligent student, but I was always driven by challenges. I made sure I got an A in every class that semester and I was also certain to let the doubters know that even though I partied with them every step of the way, I was different.

You've been criticized, ridiculed, shamed, doubted, and felt like someone else's opinion of you meant more than it should. I still can't read YouTube comments because I fear that one person will say something rude and hurtful, and I won't know how to let it go. I do know that whenever negativity comes my way, I get antsy because I treat it like the baseball pitch that I swung at and missed. But I know the next one is leaving the park. I want you to take anything that is not positive in the same light. No matter where the hurdle comes from, if it's an unexpected home repair, an argument with a relative, an issue with a coworker, it is a prelude to something outstanding in the future. Prepare for it now.

· · · · ·

Week 3 To-Do List: List three people that you can call on to vent if you feel like you can't handle what's going on in your life. Make sure they are friends or family that will not judge you and have the ability to listen. If you don't have three people, list any name you can think of and when it's time, call them.

WEEK 4

THE BAG

I want you to dream,

But I also want you to plan,

I want you to be <u>hot</u>, .

Without stressing about your <u>fans</u>,

I want you to know that no one will hand you the world, but if you put the work in, the world is inside your hands,

And when I say work, I don't mean just your employment,

I'm talking about your passion, the thing that brings you enjoyment,

'Cause I know, some days that 9-to-5 is annoying,

But it gives you the luxuries you're affording,

Keep listening,

I want you to think, but don't let it block your emotion,

I want you to envision success and put that in motion,

I want you to fail and embrace it, and kill the notion,

That it's negative to get knocked down,

'Cause see devotion, makes the journey and the struggle like drugs that get you open,

Went broke, but I wasn't broken

My fear stopped my promotion,

For years, I wasn't chosen,

Complaining to The Creator's like trying to turn back the date,

Or like teardrops to an ocean,

It's nothing,

Don't shun this because it rhymes

Just plug this inside your mind,

It's great to hustle and grind for the bag,

But don't be blind,

If the reason that you're running is strictly to get the money,

I'm not hating on your run,

But one day you'll run out of time

This was the moment I signed my record deal with Virgin Records in 2004. I was in my lawyer Matt Middleton's office with my managers KJ, Boobie, and Lenny S. I didn't receive any money that day but I was beaming with happiness about my future.

THE BAG

I want you to dream,
But I also want you to plan,
I want you to be hot,
Without stressing about your fans,

What do we really mean when we refer to dreams? Dreams often start when you're too young to do anything about them. Dreaming is similar to sitting back and fantasizing about the future while wishing for the stars to align to make your highest hopes become a reality. Dreams are understandable when you're in middle school. They can even exist in high school, but they shouldn't make it to senior year. By that time, if you're lucky enough to have pinpointed a passion, then you should begin to plan.

As always, I am speaking to myself. The idea of "being hot" is not being concerned with how fans feel about me. That is a double entendre and play on words with being hot and needing a fan and being hot as in popular and seeking a human fanatic to adore you. When you're hot, you eventually cool off. I never wanted to be hot. I wanted to be a consistent mainstay in people's hearts and minds. You should too.

I want you to know that no one will hand you the world,
But if you put the work in, the world is inside your hands,
And when I say work, I don't mean just your employment,
I'm talking about your passion, the thing that brings you enjoyment,
'Cause I know, some days that 9-to-5 is annoying,
But it gives you the luxuries you're affording,

There was once a time that I believed that working was the most important piece of the success puzzle. I thought that I had to outwork competitors and put in a tireless effort just to keep up with the people that were trying to eat to stay alive. But now I understand what work is. It's not all about the job you report to daily. It's about creating a space so that whatever task you're doing, there is joy involved. When you make meaningful moves like creating a business plan or mapping out the steps to become a chef while working somewhere else, those moves can be taxing and tedious, but ultimately rewarding.

Keep listening,
I want you to think, but don't let it block your emotion,
I want you to envision success and put that in motion,
I want you to fail and embrace it, and kill the notion,
That it's negative to get knocked down,

Emotional intelligence is one of the most underrated skills when it comes to communication. Men and women often have differences in relationships because of their vast emotional IQs. For some folks, it may be difficult for them to process, understand, and voice feelings without it triggering their brain to react with a fight response.

When I mention thinking without blocking emotion, I'm referring to the act of getting in touch with both sides of the brain. You should acknowledge your vision and plan the process but you should always pay attention to what feels good to you. If you have mapped out a schedule to begin working on a script or a podcast, be aware if every time you begin to work on it or give it thought, it feels worrisome. Those are honest emotions that should be taken seriously.

It's great to have a method to make things happen, but it's equally important to enjoy the process in some ways. And when your plan doesn't work out the way you had hoped, it shouldn't be considered a failure in any way, view those hiccups as guides to an alternative path. When you get knocked down or told no, that is the time to get excited because the path is starting to clear itself. The nays are like trash on the runway that had to be removed. The hurdles are similar to bad traffic that caused you to take an alternate route. Thank them and move on.

'Cause see devotion, makes the journey and the struggle like drugs that get you open,
Went broke, but I wasn't broken

My fear stopped my promotion,
For years, I wasn't chosen,
Complaining to The Creator's like trying to turn back the date,
Or like teardrops to an ocean,
It's nothing,

Devotion to anything is intense. Whether it's a marriage, a fraternity, or an idea, once you devote time and energy to it, the universe will balance itself out to grant a return on your investment. Devotion means putting your heart and soul in something so intently that the outcome is secondary to the effort. Don't let monetary setbacks keep you from giving energy to a deed. Don't let fear or loss halt you from excelling in any way.

Complaints are the main ingredient for unhappiness. When you complain to a higher power, it opens the door for more scenarios to complain about.

Don't shun this because it rhymes
Just plug this inside your mind,
It's great to hustle and grind for the bag,
But don't be blind,
If the reason that you're running is strictly to get the money,
I'm not hating on your run,
But one day you'll run out of time

There is nothing wrong with chasing "the bag." If you value the feeling of having money or being seen as someone who spends money freely or you feel validated when people recognize you as someone who is rich, then do what you need to do. But sometimes we are enlightened enough to know that money is not the root of evil, nor is it the answer to solve problems. It is a helpful tool that allows freedom. Money can buy cars and real estate, it can get you food to eat, shoes to wear, trips to explore, but it cannot add years to your life, it can't place joyful moments inside your memories, and it will not place love in your heart. If you had enough money to pay the bills and live leisurely without reporting to a job, what would you do with your time? Would you use it to make more money? Or would you simply enjoy the time allotted for you?

· · · · ·

Week 4 To-Do List: I want you to think about the biggest "bag" you've ever received. Write down the largest amount of money you've ever been given at one time. I mean a big check that may not even seem as big today. How did you feel? What was it for? How did you spend it? Is your life different today because of that payment? What will it take for you to receive another one like that?

WEEK 5

THE TRUTH ABOUT TIME

When I said time was worth more than money,
Some people listened like I said something explicit, and truly they didn't get it,
Someone asked me, "Yo if you did a show and when you got finished, instead
of giving you dollars, they tried to pay you in minutes, would you take it?"
I would take it, if it means more years,
More days with my fam, more joy, more tears,
More moments doesn't mean I won't have monetary gain,
It just means that I'm so grateful for breathing, I can't complain,
Then another dude said, "Yo, you always dropping lessons, like you never used
to worship dough and brag about possessions,
Homie, my kids are hungry, sometimes they eat seconds,
Real food, yo, they can't chew <u>minutes</u>, or eat <u>seconds</u>,"

I agreed with him but see I think the concept,
Of not praising dollars got taken out of context,
See when we have a salary; the work is required,
When it's your passion, all the work is inspired, So if it's long check, small
check, or no check, You still give your all,
And you don't worry 'bout the hours you put in, or if you fall,
And you might not know if what you're doing is your calling,
But if you would probably do it for free, you made the call.

The cover to my album entitled *The Calling*, released in 2012. The album featured a bunch of songs laced with indecision and honesty.

THE TRUTH ABOUT TIME

When I said time was worth more than money,
Some people listened like I said something explicit, and truly they didn't get it,

The film *In Time* with Justin Timberlake is based upon monetizing time as currency. In the movie, everyone lived 25 years and then they stopped aging physically. Each person had a clock inside their arm and it counted down days, hours, and minutes until their date of expiration. The rich had unlimited time while the poor lived day to day, trying to earn more days by any means. I watched that movie and imagined that concept becoming reality. I thought about a society where purchases were worth minutes, hours, and days of your existence. An expensive car would cost five to ten years off your life instead of $100,000 out of your account. To me, time is more valuable than any dollar amount and this cinematic tale was a brilliant way to display the true importance of each second.

We think about money as the means to purchase what we want. It puts us in elite social circles, it gives us the opportunity to travel and see the world. Money can provide the coverage we need, whether it's jewelry or clothing, and it can add extravagance to our lifestyle to make us beyond comfortable. But what if you had millions of dollars gifted to you and only 24 hours to enjoy it? Or what if you had modest money but over 100 years of life? Time will not buy trips, or cars, or food, but how important are any of these items without time? Spending money with another person is wonderful, but spending time with them is priceless.

Someone asked me, "Yo if you did a show and when you got finished, instead of giving
you dollars, they tried to pay you in minutes, would you take it?"
I would take it, if it means more years,
More days with my fam, more joy, more tears,
More moments doesn't mean I won't have monetary gain,
It just means that I'm so grateful for breathing, I can't complain,

"More moments" is a great way to describe the gift of time. Right before the Coronavirus struck the world, I was extremely grateful for my family. I was looking forward to every weekend so we could be together and then just like that, we were all forced to stay home and spend time together for months. It was surreal, frightening, and amazing all at once. But it made me think about what it means to be hypothetically paid with "minutes." I value my time as we all do. It's the reason we charge money for duties and the reason pay scales exist.

When you do a job, your pay is measured by the outcome, but more importantly, your money comes from you giving your time. Time is the most important part of the position. The numbers of hours you're "on the clock" determine your compensation. You punch in a clock and punch out. When you're not in, you take time off, when you're there longer you get overtime or time and a half. You get an annual salary spread out over a year's time. Even the entertainers of the world, the entrepreneurs, the content creators, and the people that have unhitched themselves from normal time constraints for your public pleasure still have set times to show up, perform, broadcast, and display their talents.

Then another dude said, "Yo you always dropping lessons, like you never used to worship dough and brag about possessions,
Homie, my kids are hungry, sometimes they eat seconds,
Real food, yo they can't chew <u>minutes</u>, or eat <u>seconds</u>,"

My father and mother split when I was 10 years old. I remember this because I purposely hardened my heart in an attempt to deal with a process I was unfamiliar with. Their arguing subsided and my father would stop by every Friday after work to bring me some type of fast food dinner and money for my mother, which contained my weekly allowance. At my age, the money didn't matter much, the food was always a thrill to receive, but I enjoyed seeing my dad for that short amount of time.

I knew that his presence in my home was not the best fit for their marriage even if I didn't know why. I also knew that my parents got along much better without the stress of being married to each other.

From the day he left until he passed away, my memories of him include coming to my basketball games, trying to replace my stolen football before my mother found out I took it to school, and seeing him fight cancer weeks before his death. I remember calling him from college just to say hello. By that time, he had remarried and had three more children. Our conversations were awkward, I became a bit resentful, and I started to realize that I didn't get to know him as an adult. My father was a provider, and I cannot take away any effort he, or my mother made, to put food on the table and clothes on my back. But as I was driving down to North Carolina for his funeral back in 2003, all I could think about was the time I missed out on. I visited my siblings and asked to look at old photo albums just so I could see the times they shared. I looked at those photo albums and saw a life that I wasn't a part of. The pictures of my dad and his "new" family reminded me that I was fortunate to have meaningful memories of him but I was somewhat disheartened that I missed out on years of new conversations, keepsakes, and mementos. The times we share and the moments we experience are the true joys of this life we are living.

I agreed with him but see I think the concept,
Of not praising dollars got taken out of context,
See when we have a salary; the work is required,
When it's your passion, all the work is inspired,

The line about salaries actually came from motivational speaker Inky Johnson. I took his words and created this piece around them. The key to this statement is that your job and your passion can mutually exist. You can truly love what you do and not have it feel like a burden each day that you work. There are educators who enjoy molding young lives. There are custodians who find satisfaction in cleaning an area. Find yours.

So if it's long check, small check, or no check,
You still give your all,
And you don't worry 'bout the hours you put in, or if you fall,
And you might not know if what you're doing is your calling,
But if you would probably do it for free, you made the call.

I did an entire music project called *The Calling*. I was completely befuddled by my lack of progress in my music career and I had reached a point of frustration. Instead of battling that feeling, I opted to nurture the indecision and ward off the despair. I embraced the unknown and created songs that highlighted the fact that I had invested so much time into "making it" that I no longer knew what "making it" was. I questioned my true calling because I didn't feel like music was filling me with the same adoration. I didn't even know how I wanted to use my voice. So with that, I had to ask myself what did I see myself doing to make a living that would fulfill me. And the answer was more than one clear-cut choice. I knew I would always write. And I knew I wanted to reach the youth and affect some lives. But most of all, I found comfort in being uncomfortable.

· · · · ·

Week 5 To-Do List: If money was not an issue and you hit the lottery for an unreal, ever-flowing amount, what would you wake up and do everyday that would bring you joy? What job would bring you passion if the financial return didn't matter? Ask yourself, write down the answer or answers, and make sure you are on the path to that particular career, job, or daily regimen that aligns with your happy place.

Now answer the same question with time being the non-factor. What if you didn't have an earthly checkout time and you could slowly attain your goals? If death were not in the near future, or possibly the future at all, what would you do with your day?

WEEK 6

THE ONE

A lot of us are searching for the one with that connection,
The person perfect for you doesn't mean they are perfection,
They make you smile inside,
When they're around it lifts your vibe to be the greatest version of yourself,
they brighten your reflection,
But to make a thing go right, it really takes two,
In order to attract that magic, you must be great too,
So while you're rating all your dates, the critical breakthrough,
Is looking in the mirror and asking you would you date you?
The mirror told me, "No," but I was too ashamed to own it,
It's hard to tell the truth, when you don't really know it,
Someone told me love is not a feeling but an action,
You can have it, but it's tragic not to find a way to show it,
So what's your insecurity?
Is it your anatomy?
A body part? The hair on your head?
Are you a casualty of past heartbreak?
Is your weight causing catastrophe?
So now you think that you don't deserve something that's hassle-free,
Beautiful and worthy of risking a broken heart,
It's cool to take the risk, but don't skip the important part,
A lot of us are damaged,
And we try to heal gunshot wounds with a bandage,
The dawn is close to the dark,
We all want to find that one, so we pursue,
A counterpart, partner to make us feel fresh and new,
Before you judge somebody else, be sure to improve yourself,
And ask one last time, is "The One" looking for you?

My wife and I were engaged twice. This 2011 photo shoot was the first engagement shoot and it was bitter cold even though we got some great shots. We ended up calling off the wedding in 2012 so we could find ourselves before finding each other again. We're truly blessed.

THE ONE

A lot of us are searching for the one with that connection,
The person perfect for you doesn't mean they are perfection,
They make you smile inside,
When they're around it lifts your vibe to be the greatest version of yourself, they
brighten your reflection,

An elder in my family that has been married for over 50 years gave me his thoughts on building a lasting relationship and finding someone perfect. He told me "the one" is really the person in the mirror and in our lives, there are counterparts, companions, and partners that we meet along the path that we connect with at certain points in life.

He said the person you date when you're 24 might not be a match for you when you're 31, but it doesn't mean they weren't right at the time. Then there comes a moment when there's a person that you find that you would like to share your bloodline, time, thoughts, memories, finances, family, and space with.

"The one" suggests that it's the perfect match. That she meets him and he meets her and no one can break their bond, nothing can wrong their right, they are no longer searching for the one; they are one.

I understood.

But to make a thing go right, it really takes two,
In order to attract that magic, you must be great too,
So while you're rating all your dates, the critical breakthrough,
Is looking in the mirror and asking you would you date you?

This is a tough question at times. The confident, assertive person swiftly answers yes. It makes sense that if you believe you are a great catch, then you probably are. But if you're unsure about your financial space or your appearance, then you might not be so quick to jump at the chance to date yourself. The issue that arises with the question I've asked is that most of us won't ask it, and if we did, we would only be as honest as possible. It doesn't mean we'd lie to ourselves. It means that for a person to say that he or she is "undateable," then they would have to unpack the baggage and peel back the layers to find the root of the reason and how your undesirable traits developed over time. Who wants to really do that unless you're laying on someone's couch in therapy? It's much easier to say, "Hell yes, I would be lucky to date myself."

The mirror told me, "No," but I was too ashamed to own it,
It's hard to tell the truth, when you don't really know it,
Someone told me love is not a feeling but an action,
You can have it, but it's tragic not to find a way to show it,

When the mirror told me "no," it was because my skin was bad, my money was "funny," my confidence was shaky, and I had not gotten in touch with Sherod for almost a decade. People think monikers, alter egos, and even work names don't mean anything, but they do. When I was in middle school, I was Sherod. I was a bit shy, awkward, smart, and I desired popularity. When I started high school, I was still Sherod but I could feel my identity switching once I made the basketball team and classmates knew my name. By the time I was a senior, everyone called me Sha. Sha was much cooler, mildly athletic, not as smart, but way more popular. College was similar to my senior year of high school, except I was on the Dean's List and basketball slowly faded from the picture. And then there was the industry life where Sha Stimuli was born.

I walked around with that title for almost 12 years before I became "Mr. Williams" at work, "Coach Williams" when I coached basketball, "Sherod" when I met new people, and I was still "Sha" on the basketball court. For the first time in many years, I was introducing myself as Sherod. I wasn't sure how Sherod would be received if no one knew that I was a gifted emcee. I wanted to always be appreciated for my talent, but when I arrived at a school and joined the ranks of the educators, I was starting from scratch as a man with a clean slate. I had to get to know myself as this person before I could exist in a relationship with someone else.

No one would seriously date a person that has no clue who they are.

As far as love goes, I agree that it is an action word but it doesn't always involve deeds. Sometimes the action is a constant thought about an individual that you're interested in. Love is so powerful that by the time you realize you're in it, you've already acted like a fool in love repeatedly.

So what's your insecurity?
Is it your anatomy?
A body part? The hair on your head?
Are you a casualty of past heartbreak?
Is your weight causing catastrophe?
So now you think that you don't deserve something that's hassle-free,
Beautiful and worthy of risking a broken heart,
It's cool to take the risk, but don't skip the important part,

I told you my insecurities. One of the ones that stuck with me for my entire life was my weight. I was called skinny, bony, lanky, and every name in the book when I was little, so as a grown man weighing over 200 pounds, I still see a slim kid that didn't necessarily get teased often, but my self-image was distorted. Some of you have weight issues and no matter what you do, you can't seem to commit to losing pounds. The moment that you're looking for is not far off. It happens when you realize that any change you need to make in your lifestyle in regards to exercise, health, or eating will only take place when you want them to. And it won't be for some superficial reason. It will simply hit you that there is another version of you that hasn't shown its face yet. For me, I wanted to be a muscular, chiseled, broad man but since I didn't work out enough and my fast metabolism kept the weight off, I would wear baggy clothes to hide my frame. There was a new Sherod that wanted to meet the world and his physique wasn't his best attribute. His looks were one aspect of his confidence, his levels of honesty he exhibited, and his way of life. The person that you are going to be once you choose to make some different decisions is probably happier, friendlier, and that individual is most likely more physically fit than you are now. What's even crazier is that there's an even better version of me that I haven't been introduced to yet. I'm thrilled about it.

A lot of us are damaged,
And we try to heal gunshot wounds with a bandage,
The dawn is close to the dark,
We all want to find that one, so we pursue,
A counterpart, partner to make us feel fresh and new,
Before you judge somebody else, be sure to improve yourself,
And ask one last time, is "The One" looking for you?

Some people look for a magical, spiritual connection that wondrously flows and happens without thinking, where two hearts join and mirror each other without a conscious effort because they are predestined soul mates.

Is that what you believe? That God intervened in the beginning and made everyone in the form of couples?

Does that even sound real?

And what if you made babies and shared vows already? Is it your partner's fault that your relationship is not full of bliss?

What are we really saying by labeling someone Mr. or Mrs. Right? Assuming that there's a right person means that everyone other than that person is incorrect. Maybe there isn't a match for us all. Maybe we just find a great percentage of what we like in a human and write off the rest as characteristics we don't mind putting up with.

All of this pontification brings us back to where we started. Imagine finding the one human who makes you smile from the inside out, someone who checks every box and ignites every fiber of your existence. If that person were to get to know you, how would they feel about you? Do your energies sync up at all? Are you in a place that would turn people off because you're so driven to be successful, or you're focused on your kids, or maybe you are still scorned from the last relationship and you need time to heal? You could just be in a place where you've been alone for so long that you don't know how to trust or open up. Whatever the answer is, it is important to recognize where you are and what vibe you are giving off to the world.

If the one you are supposed to end up with is looking for you as well, then you two will find each other. And at that time, the signs will continue to point toward the feeling in your soul when you think of that person, or when you know you're about to see them, or talk to them, or you miss them. Some of you have felt this more than once and you wonder if you're confusing novelty butterflies with true deep connection. The feeling of newness attacks your heart and your head. You can almost feel yourself wondering how long the fluttery feeling will last. But when your soul is awakened, there isn't a chance to question if something is real. Your soul doesn't care about heartbreak or logical decisions. It is only interested in growing closer to another soul and experiencing elation. Your focus, as cliché as it might sound, is to prepare yourself for the opportunity.

If you can hold onto one thing from this entire rant about finding love with another person, remember that dating is not an audition. You are not in a position to judge someone to detect if they are suitable to be by your side. Getting to know someone is a chance and an opportunity for you to express your feelings for someone else, show them how you would like to be treated by your actions, and to slowly find commonalities and lower communication barriers to reveal each other's true selves until you've reached the highest levels of trust, honesty, and, possibly, love.

· · · · ·

Week 6 To-Do List: If you're single, answer the question…would you date yourself? If not, why wouldn't you?

If you're in a serious, committed relationship or a marriage, do you feel like you are with the one?

Lastly, list all the qualities that make you perfectly imperfect.

Write down the attributes that make you a "catch" and the parts of you that need work. Here's an example:

Gifts	Under Construction
Tall	Finances
Kind	Follow-through
Funny	Thoughtfulness
Intelligent	Egotistical
Good cook	Holds grudges
Great hygiene	Insecure
Prompt	Trust issues
Flexible	Argumentative
	Commitment phobia

WEEK 7

THE LADDER

I'm in a space where all hate and shade gets rejected,
All criticism deflected,
The way I'm feeling today, I'm angelic, blessed and protected,
When devils enter my section attempting to use their method,
To conjure curses I'm perfectly shielded and unaffected,
But I wasn't always like this,
Matter of fact, I remember the time,
When I got overdraft fees, after blowing mad cheese,
It was like my whole existence took a heavy decline,
I don't think it's rock bottom, but an evident sign,
Is when you speak like the stars won't ever align,
What people call "The good life," I said would never be mine,
Then the extreme is that it's better to die,
But one day…
Not only did I decide that I wanted to live,
With all that I was taking on, I still wanted to give,
So I was mentoring, coaching, and building with kids,
It didn't happen overnight, but it felt like it did,
So I gave God the glory,
Y'all couldn't see, the internal battle was gory,
But peep this,
Everything happening to me, it was part of my story,
And it wasn't happening to me, it was happening for me,
So please know the difference between the former and latter,
And start stepping on hurdles until you're forming a ladder

My substitute teacher ID. This was a defining moment in my life that humbled me and prepared me to become a better individual.

THE LADDER

I'm in a space where all hate and shade gets rejected,
All criticism deflected,
The way I'm feeling today, I'm angelic, blessed and protected,
When devils enter my section attempting to use their method,
To conjure curses I'm perfectly shielded and unaffected,

That sounds like a beautiful place to be in. No hate can bother me, no criticism can damage me; no curses or negative thoughts can alter my path. This feeling of spiritual shielding goes hand-in-hand with evolution. To reach this point in your life, it takes constant practice of positive thoughts. Even when adversity hits, or someone throws offensive words to get you rattled, you find a way to morph it into goodness.

One of the scenarios I like to refer to is the day when one of my co-workers attempted to question my integrity. This person was somewhat of a supervisor and the attempt was via an email chain that went directly up to the person in charge of the school I worked at. Can you imagine being in a space of joy and peace and then finding out someone wants to assassinate your character? Even though I felt the instant need to handle the situation with anger and to provide glaring proof to clear my name, I simply spoke directly to the person with a calm demeanor so it would not seem like a confrontation. I used the word "simply" but it wasn't easy to talk myself into a rational mode and to ask myself why I attracted this type of energy at my workplace. I continued to probe and figure out what role I played in this incident. The more I looked within, the less perturbed I was. I knew that whatever accusations were headed my way, they were not meant for me at all.

But I wasn't always like this,
Matter of fact, I remember the time,
When I got overdraft fees, after blowing mad cheese,
It was like my whole existence took a heavy decline,

For someone's entire existence to take a decline is a heavy statement. When I was a single man bringing in a spotty income, I was consistently overdrafting my bank account, and I did not see a way out of the situation I was in.

One evening in 2012, I was in the grocery store pinching pennies and grabbing necessities and I suddenly started to feel sorry for myself. I began daydreaming and I flashed back to being backstage at a Jay-Z concert in New York City. My daydream led me to the year 2004 when I had the mindset that I was going to be center stage at Madison Square Garden in the future. Kanye West spoke to me briefly and said he wanted to do some music for my album but he needed to know my budget. T.I. remembered me from my days of running around Atlanta trying to get a record deal back in 2001 and he took a picture with me. Beyoncé introduced herself and shook my hand and I was very cool with all of Jay-Z's security and his stylist June Ambrose.

My mind was reliving the glory days until a cashier told me I was next in line and I instantly bounced back into reality. I sneakily pulled out my Public Assistance card, also known as food stamps. I wasn't sure how much I had on the card but it was enough to cover my groceries. I walked to the parking lot with a cart full of items and I spotted a familiar face near the exit. It was a rap artist I grew up listening to standing in the parking lot talking to another dude. I kept staring at him trying to make sure it was him. I had no idea he lived in Atlanta because I knew he was from the projects in Bedford Stuyvesant, Brooklyn. I said his name with a soft tone and uncertainty, he looked up, said, "What up?" and then gave me a pound (handshake). I told him that I patterned my style after him when I was a kid, and that his fast rapping flow was one that I wanted to master. I also mentioned that I was cool with one of his former partners. I was about to walk away, and then it hit me, "Yo we have a song together!" I told him my name was Stimuli, and my homeboy PR put us on a song together. I don't know if he recalled the song but he pulled me to the side and asked if he could talk to me. My mind was wandering, trying to figure out what he might want. I looked stunned and confused. He spoke in almost a low whisper and went into details about being evicted and needing some money until his next publishing check came in. I wasn't sure if his story was fiction or not, but I took my bags to my car, went back inside the supermarket and took out $40 from the ATM. I walked back outside, gave him a pound and dropped the money in his hand. Moments later I got a message from my bank. I had overdrafted my account. For some reason I wasn't upset, I felt like it was important for me to give and I knew the money would come back to me. Two days later, my friend Jason called me and told me he was moving into my apartment complex and he gave my name as the person that referred him. My rent was going to be waived for the next month because of that referral. I was reminded that I was blessed.

I don't think it's rock bottom, but an evident sign,
Is when you speak like the stars won't ever align,
What people call "The good life," I said would never be mine,
Then the extreme is that it's better to die,

This is difficult for me to articulate because I don't think people understand how depression really works. I did not hit rock bottom. There were no intense drug moments or self-harm. There were simply thoughts. That's it.

I allowed thoughts inside my head that led me to believe that my life had seen its best days. I thought that the only way I would get credit and praise for everything I'd done musically up to that point was to be memorialized. I had to die for someone to care. That was my thought process. And it started as a fleeting thought. Then it increased to thinking about the best way to go without pain. Then it turned up more and I thought, if I don't care about dying, I should sell drugs full-time, or maybe do a big crime to get notoriety. Suicide was out of the question, but it doesn't mean it didn't cross my mind.

I would often drift off and play out these situations in my head where people would say admirable things about my characteristics after I was gone. They would find the hidden gems in my songs and my words would make it to classrooms and museums. These visions existed with the one common chilling factor that was indeed my own demise. I didn't plan on being around to enjoy the love I would eventually get, but that didn't matter to me at the time. It sounds foolish and maybe a little insane, but it was honestly a daily way of thinking and processing my transition out of the music business. When my friend Rhian Stoute was murdered in New Jersey, I remember being with him days prior to his death. Not only did I feel like I could've easily been with him the day his fake friend decided to rob and kill him, but also I almost envied the admiration he received after he passed. It was an eerie series of mental ups and downs that I was going through. I was fortunate to be alive but bothered that my life felt pointless. Depression can come in many forms. Mine was subtle, but it was still real.

But one day…
Not only did I decide that I wanted to live,
With all that I was taking on, I still wanted to give,
So I was mentoring, coaching, and building with kids,
It didn't happen overnight, but it felt like it did,

The path to working in the schools was not straightforward and it wasn't received with open arms. Many years ago, I did an interview and I was asked what I would be doing if I wasn't making music and I said I would most likely be a teacher. I said that because I could not see myself waking up working for anyone other than myself or to push forward humanity. Then I said that I wouldn't be satisfied being at one school all day, so I told the interviewer that I would want to be a teacher on tour (similar to a substitute teacher). I didn't know where I was going with that but it was a bit of foreshadowing.

Teachers mean a lot to us all. We all have some we remember and some we'd like to forget. For me, I wanted to be the reason some youngsters felt motivated to do better in life. I got that opportunity when I sat in a classroom as a substitute for a team-taught class with the basketball coach at North Springs High School in Atlanta.

Carlos Cliett was a science teacher at North Springs at that time. He was cool and calm in the classroom, and after a few times being in his room covering for his special education team teacher we spoke briefly about life and basketball. I knew two of his players that played with me at LA Fitness in the Sandy Springs neighborhood so I asked about them, he pulled out his computer, and asked me to watch a varsity game so I could see them play. I did. I had comments and questions. He asked where I played college ball, and I offered assistance if he needed it. He said he might be able to use me. I showed up to every practice that summer and invited my boy Kendrick Reid along when the season started because Carlos needed a freshmen coach as well as an assistant. And so it began. I knew very little about strategy and how to prepare students for games. But I knew I wanted the best for these young men and I was dedicated to that. My life has more meaning and purpose because of that choice to become a coach.

So I gave God the glory,
Y'all couldn't see, the internal battle was gory,
But peep this,
Everything happening to me, it was part of my story,
And it wasn't happening to me, it was happening for me,
So please know the difference between the former and latter,
And start stepping on hurdles until you're forming a ladder

What I've described to you is a short part of a long journey that felt trying at times. In the midst of it there was indecision, fear, pain, and an inner voice that guided me when I didn't know which move was right. Everything that I thought was happening to me was strengthening me. I can honestly point to every obstruction and stumbling block and see exactly how it made me more resilient and added clarity. The hardships became helpful. My message to you is to turn the hurdles into ladder steps. I know I talked about pressure and wins and lessons, but this is about embracing the situation and using it as a platform to elevate your life.

· · · · ·

Week 7 To-Do List: List your losses that seemed to cripple your world when they happened. Think about how you handled them, what got you through, and how you turned each hurdle into a ladder step.

WEEK 8

THE REJECTION

I always knew I had a gift; this is a "Godsent" flow,

So I prayed for rap supremacy,

He said, "Nah, let go."

And that sparked some crazy stress which uncovered amazing blessings,

Then somebody asked the question, "What if God says no?"

I thought that's dumb,

He's supposed to answer prayers,

Be a child protector, house provider, sickness, cancer slayer,

Throw us money, fix relationships, we call him, He should show up,

Especially if we go to church, He should be Santa Claus for grownups right?

Wrong? I guess that I'm a living witness,

I was pushing, grinding, working, trying to run the music business,

But I had to realize that when you get so much resistance,

God is using redirection, GPS just switched the distance,

This is where you have to listen,

See the destination's different,

I was typing in a "place," it got rerouted to a mission,

I was focused on fame, praise, financial wealth,

Upset when it wasn't coming, had to humble myself,

So what are you gonna do when The Creator says no?

But She needs you to keep going, She's throwing you something else,

That's way better than anything you can conceive,

When a challenge hits your calendar, will you still believe?

In 2003, I was featured in the Unsigned Hype section of *The Source Magazine*. Back then this was a big deal. I'm still proud of this accomplishment. I thought stardom was around the corner.

THE REJECTION

I always knew I had a gift; this is a "Godsent" flow,
So I prayed for rap supremacy,
He said, "Nah, let go."
And that sparked some crazy stress which uncovered amazing blessings,
Then somebody asked the question, "What if God says no?"

This was one of the most difficult truths for me to accept when I was deep in the middle of my journey to become a superstar. Even today when I watch documentaries on hip-hop, or I speak to people about my missteps, there is a twinge of "what if?" that roams around in my head. No matter how talented I might have been, no matter how kind I was to people, and even though my heart was in the game for all the right reasons, I still made moves that landed me where I am today. And when I was making those moves, it felt like my life was falling apart. I could not understand why God would allow me to get close to my dream and then snatch it away. I assumed it wasn't fair.

I thought that's dumb,
He's supposed to answer prayers,
Be a child protector, house provider, sickness, cancer slayer,
Throw us money, fix relationships, we call him, He should show up,
Especially if we go to church, he should be Santa Claus for grownups right?

We all view God in different ways. But for the most part, we believe that if we humbly request a minor miracle or spiritual intervention, there is a direct line to The Creator. But what happens when there is no miracle? Would you stop believing because you weren't rewarded? God is the voice that talks to you silently. He is the one asking questions and checking on you. But some of us have a habit of asking God for help when it's needed. At the times we face rejection, we have to acknowledge the fact that rent might not be on time because the universe is preparing a house. A job may feel frustrating because the new position is being worked out. A re-

lationship might just fall off so that another human can find their way to
your heart.

Wrong? I guess that I'm a living witness,
I was pushing, grinding, working, trying to run the music business,
But I had to realize that when you get so much resistance,
God is using <u>redirection, GPS just switched the distance</u>,

God is using you and sometimes there needs to be some type of rerouting.
When you get a "no," that is a trigger to make a move and get excited because
something is on the way. I think about my life when I read these few bars. I
always wanted to make music so that I could live free, change lives, and express myself. But the main part was to connect with people that I would not
meet. I knew where my end destination was but God put me on a different
path to get there and I almost gave up a few times. The feeling when you
break through your own mental barrier is amazing.

This is where you have to listen,
See the <u>destination's different</u>,
I was typing in a <u>"place," it got rerouted to a mission</u>,
I was focused on fame, praise, financial wealth,
Upset when it wasn't coming, had to humble myself,

I assumed success looked a certain way and that it felt like reaching a final pla-
teau. But there's no finality when you want to be famous. It's a full-time job
that continues until the fans decide otherwise. I wanted to be held in high regards by strangers across the globe. I forgot about my original mission to reach
people once I felt rejection from the industry. I started to mention my lack of
money, popularity, credit, accolades, and anything else that would sound self-
deprecating when I was composing songs.

So what are you gonna do when The Creator says no?
But She needs you to keep going, She's throwing you something else,
That's way better than anything you can conceive,

When a challenge hits your calendar, will you still believe?

The difference between a loss and a rejection is the rejection often feels like you placed the key to your contentment in someone else's hands and they tossed the key away.

This is for the people that may be right in that rough patch, that sunken place, that black hole that seems to have zero light near. Trust in yourself before you listen to these words. There is a plan, and you are in control of it. Switch your energy.

· · · · ·

Week 8 To-Do List: Think about the time when someone said no to a request that was very instrumental in your life. Was there a time where a bad break like a lost job, or an ended relationship, or some type of heartache seemed like you had no control over the outcome? Maybe it was in high school or early in your adulthood but it made you the person you are today. How did that rejection make you feel? Why was this person given the power to deny you and did it make you work harder?

WEEK 9

THE MEDICINE

When life gets real, how do you deal?
When you don't want to feel, how do you deal?
Some people smoke "loud," other folks pop pills,
Me, I used to drink the pain away, and eat unhappy meals,
Fast food kills, nicotine is ill,
Hard liquor deads your liver, but we love the way it feels,
If I was 16 or 17, I can keep it real,
If my homies were on "lean," then my cup would be filled,
With that Dirty Sprite, purple stuff, friends would tell me chill,
But if I had a little job and I ain't have a lot of bills,
I'd be self-medicating with my health steady fading,
It wouldn't help when I take it, but the pain would be concealed,

Right now a kid somewhere is battling depression,
Someone's getting bullied online in a comment section,
Some young teens are lighting up daily before class,
And the "Xannies" make the dreadful days and nights go by fast,
So how do I tell my sons there's a way that's legit,
To handle stress, anxiety, and craziness fits?
See we live in a world where a song with the chorus screaming, "Molly, Per-cocet," was a radio hit,
Back in the days it was, "How High" and "Mary Jane,"
We always glorified using, as the tool to keep us sane,
I don't know what your vice is,
But I pray and hope; it's not worth more than your life is,
Find a way to cope...please

Poppin' bottles in 2006 with my brother Lord Digga, and my boys Kijana El-cock and Andre Cooper are also pictured here. We were in a VIP section for one of my two birthday parties that year. This was my life at the time.

THE MEDICINE

When life gets real, how do you deal?
When you don't want to feel, how do you deal?
Some people smoke "loud," other folks pop pills,
Me, I used to drink the pain away, and eat unhappy meals,

When I was a child, I often wondered why adults drank beer. I tasted it and I remember being disgusted by the bitterness. I asked my father multiple times for a solid reason why he drank those Pink Champales. He just laughed it off as if I would find out the answer one day.

Peer pressure got the best of me in high school, and I found myself sharing 40-ounce beers just to fit in while hoping I didn't throw up. It wasn't until I got to college that I associated alcohol with lowered inhibitions and a bit of mindlessness. As I got older, I saw functioning alcoholism time and time again, and frequently my peers were enablers. Seeing grown men abuse the bottle was sad, but as friends of abusers, we weren't mature enough to intervene. I made a rule with myself that I would never submit to any vice. I thank God that life has never allowed me to feel so defeated that I wanted to be numb on a daily basis. My healthy way of dealing with stress is basketball, exercise, and if I do need an elixir, it is not enough to damage my senses. I wasn't always so headstrong.

Fast food kills, nicotine is ill,
Hard liquor deads your liver, but we love the way it feels,

There was a time when fast food was consistently a part of my diet, and Hennessy Cognac was my social medicine. "Henny" was the cure for mental pain and a way to briefly escape from reality. In college, it was the perfect complement to an otherwise boring evening. I became somewhat dependent on cognac to open me up and make me humorous, friendly, or even likable. In my adult years after postsecondary education, liquor became synonymous with weekends, parties, and any social event with the opposite gender. I can count on one hand the times that I actually got sick from alcohol, but I did realize that I was drinking to tap into a version of myself with more personality. I wanted to be more talkative and I wanted people to view me as fun because without sipping a liqueur, I felt bland and lame. I didn't see that this was an unhealthy way of viewing myself until many years later as I approached 40 years on the planet.

Becoming a parent didn't completely sober me up, but it did add a new type of joy that deterred me from seeking numbness. For everyone that hugs the bottle as an outlet, the key is moderation. If you are a functioning alcoholic, you may not have a clue, even though your family and friends are probably tiptoeing around the subject. But if you feel like a spirited beverage is what you crave in order to survive every 24 hours, you may consider speaking to someone.

If I was 16 or 17, I can keep it real,
If my homies were on "lean," then my cup would be filled,
With that Dirty Sprite, purple stuff, friends would tell me chill,
But if I had a little job and I ain't have a lot of bills,
I'd be self-medicating with my health steady fading,
It wouldn't help when I take it, but the pain would be concealed,

As a young basketball player in Flatbush, Brooklyn, we played in the parks religiously when it got warm. Our summer mornings were spent at McDonald's or a diner, and then on the basketball courts before the sun started blazing. We usually had tournament games in the evening and even if we didn't, we were playing all day.

I'm bringing this up because I distinctly remember those mornings where I would walk to the park to play with guys like Kijana or Paul and there would be guys from the neighborhood there as early as 8 a.m. sitting on the benches. They were usually rolling up weed or they had a beer in a brown paper bag. Some of them were in their 30s, sometimes there were high school kids that were a few years older than us. They would speak to us and give salutations.

Sometimes we would see guys that were former ball players sitting on benches looking like the personification of a dream deferred.

It seemed like kids had to choose what lane they were going to ride in. Either you were a ballplayer, a homebody, a street dude, or a "weedhead." "Weed-heads" talked slowly, their moves were lethargic, and their lives seemed to be lagging a few paces behind everyone else. Even though some really great basketball players were avid tree smokers, there were other guys who dedicated their existence to puffing cannabis. I never wanted to be one of those dudes in the park that looked extremely sleepy all the time and smelled like sativa. They wanted to smoke marijuana for breakfast before they even consumed food.

But if I were a teen in today's world, listening to today's music, I'm not so sure I would be able to steer clear of the pitfalls. Social media, music, and movies are all heavy influencers today. It will take some careful dedication and focus to keep my two boys from seeking intoxicants to help them handle life's curveballs.

Right now a kid somewhere is battling depression,
Someone's getting bullied online in a comment section,
Some young teens are lighting up daily before class,
And the "Xannies" make the dreadful days and nights go by fast,

Most of the fights I see in the public school system stem from comments made on a social media post. It was weird at first when I used to break up a fight and try to get to the origin of the altercation. Someone would most likely say that the beef began over a post and a comment that was almost always deleted. But of course there was a screenshot going around and the flames just got higher and hotter. For most of us, we post our thoughts online and when we get push-back, we handle it with class. But imagine being young and not having any guidance or precedence to know what to do.

So if a child becomes the victim of mass shaming on social media, it can be detrimental to their psyche. A posted fight or an embarrassing moment can cause a young person to feel like the world is too much for them. In some cases, they turn to pills, in other cases; they choose to exit the earth. I have as many deep conversations that I can with students that are in pain but there is no way to be sure that the intervention is working.

So how do I tell my sons there's a way that's legit,
To handle stress, anxiety, and craziness fits?
See we live in a world where a song with the chorus screaming, "Molly, Percocet,"
was a radio hit,
Back in the days it was, "How High" and "Mary Jane,"
We always glorified using, as the tool to keep us sane,
I don't know what your vice is,
But I pray and hope; it's not worth more than your life is,
Find a way to cope...please!

Of course I would love to use athletics as a way to keep my boys distracted from everything under the sun that will hit them during their adolescent years, but that is just a small part of the process that lies ahead. The most challenging and probably the most important factor that will assist my wife and I while we raise young kings will be creating a soft, safe landing space for them. That means that we have to maintain a home where honesty is valued and openness is met without judgment. Drugs are not going to vanish from our society and alcohol will always be a rite of passage for adolescents.

Somehow, I want to let them and every young person in the world know that life is all about making choices. I want them to read or listen to former NBA champion Lamar Odom's book, *Darkness to Light*. Lamar goes into detail about loss and how he dealt with severe emotional pain. I want my sons to know that we all cope differently and hearing some of the tragic lows that tormented Lamar can serve as an eye opener. Lamar dealt with his mom passing from cancer when he was young, he had to continue playing basketball after his baby died at six months of age, and his struggle with cocaine and addiction are all valuable lessons to me. I hope my guys will get something from it.

• • • • •

Week 9 To-Do List: Almost all of us have vices and stress relievers from drugs and alcohol to food and sex. Identify a few of the outlets you chose ten years ago and the ones you choose now. Write them down next to each other and analyze how you've grown and continue to grow. If you're in your twenties, go back five years. An example:

Ten Years Ago	Today
Basketball	Exercise
Drinking	Meditation
Partying	Occasional drink
Smoking	Conversation with my wife
Fast Food	Breakfast food

WEEK 10

THE LAW OF ATTRACTION

I remember reading the book called *The Secret*,
Speaking things into existence, I had to try it,
Had a dollar bill with six zeros taped to my ceiling,
Either *The Secret* didn't work, or I didn't know how to apply it,
I thought that I'd wake up to my desires,
I've seen so many ride until their <u>wheels fall off</u>, then they <u>re-tire</u>,
We all know people that are happy to be hired, They complain about their job, and then they're mad when they get fired,
The law of attraction that I spoke of near the intro,
It's hard to keep it going when your income's coming in slow,
And then you add <u>offspring</u>, that need you all seasons and you can't take <u>off spring</u>, life can be exhausting,
So how did I master it?
That's what you're asking,
Instead of hoping and wishing,
I envisioned already having it,
I did it with my possessions, I even did it with my marriage,
I remember tapping into the feeling, not just imagining,
A wife and a child, but how they would add to happiness,
And now we keep adding, like practicing mathematics,
The family is expanding,
Career moves we were planning,
Are coming into fruition,
By simply just understanding,
Got a bigger house and whip, and I promise that I'm not bragging,
The secret is be joyful without it, then you attract it

My engineer Amond Jackson snapped this photo while I was in the recording booth and Azizi came to sit in on a session in 2015. I was finally proud of the music I was making and I wanted to share it with her. Zaire was in her stomach listening. This photo inspired the album cover for my *Lazarus* album released in 2017.

THE LAW OF ATTRACTION

I remember reading the book called The Secret,
Speaking things into existence, I had to try it,
Had a dollar bill with six zeros taped to my ceiling,
Either The Secret *didn't work, or I didn't know how to apply it,*

The first time I heard about *The Secret*, it was back in 2008. A few of my friends raved about it and my former manager came to my house to hand me a copy of the movie. I guess he felt like I needed it more than he did so I watched it a few times. The first few minutes I was skeptical because I didn't believe that I could play a part in redirecting the outcome of my downward spiraling life. The idea of visualizing desires made sense to me, but as logical as it was, it seemed difficult. I didn't realize how negative my thoughts and writing were before I saw the film. After watching the film, I started using more positive thoughts and I began expecting better outcomes.

I recorded a whole mixtape entitled *The Secret* and it was dedicated to positive affirmations. I then put a dollar bill with six handwritten zeros on my ceiling in my bedroom. The same bedroom that my big brother spent his high school years in had become mine once I graduated from college and moved back home. I was sleeping in a twin bed in my mother's home, I had reached the frightening age of 30, and the dollar bill that I stared at every morning when I first opened my eyes was supposed to magically transform into one million in my bank account. It did not.

I thought that I'd wake up to my desires,
I've seen so many ride until their <u>wheels fall off</u>, then they <u>re-tire</u>,
We all know people that are happy to be hired,
They complain about their job, and then they're mad when they get fired,

At the time I saw that movie, I didn't have a job, but I was around people that were gainfully employed. I envied their ability to wake up daily and perform duties to live their adorable lives. It was cute to me, and I say that in the most condescending way because that was how clueless I was.

I thought my method of staying with my mother and being broke for years was "the way." I just knew it would pay off years later. I knew people that worked city jobs for years and years so they would have stability, and I knew others that complained about having to work but they didn't do anything about it. I couldn't understand either position. I really believed I wasn't being lazy by avoiding employment. I was a freelance writer for magazines and I earned dollars at temp jobs but I didn't want anything that would cause me to be at a specific location daily.

Now that I've had years to analyze what I honestly felt, I can see that I was filled with fear. I was abnormally afraid that my flexibility would be snatched away if I had to truly earn for myself. That was an entitled, spoiled, and unrealistic way of approaching adulthood, but that was who I was at the time.

The law of attraction that I spoke of near the intro,
It's hard to keep it going when your income's coming in slow,
And then you add offspring, that need you all seasons and you can't take off spring,
life can be exhausting,

Aside from friends that I knew with jobs, I also knew those with kids. And when you mention the law of attraction to someone that's working at a place they don't love, or living somewhere that isn't glamorous while they raise their offspring, they don't want to hear about any magic tricks or secret laws. What works is what's in front of them. I tried not to fall victim to that narrow-minded view of the world. Visualization seemed to work for parking spots, and it was easy to anticipate empty seats at the movie theater. *The Secret*, however, was only working for rich people. That's what I believed.

So how did I master it?
That's what you're asking,
Instead of hoping and wishing,

I envisioned already having it,
I did it with my possessions, I even did it with my marriage,
I remember tapping into the feeling, not just imagining,
A wife and a child, but how they would add to happiness,

A few years ago, I started a process I call Rearview Gratitude. It started the day my fiancé Azizi and I decided to move in together for the second time after living apart for almost two years.

We got back together and we were trying to get an apartment but we kept getting denied. I didn't officially have a job and she had an old bill on her credit that needed to be taken care of, so our credit scores weren't strong enough to get the type of place we were applying for. We thought about moving into my apartment complex and getting a two-bedroom, but after visiting some of the newer complexes with renovations and amenities, we wanted something better. We were about to be married, and even though it was important to save for a house, we both wanted a fresh start in a new spot that we could call our own.

We sat in a Chick-Fil-A restaurant and we ate and felt a little dejected and somewhat lost. But we both silently felt a feeling that was new to us and in hindsight, I realize what we felt was acceptance. It was surreal. It was as though we had been through so much separately that no new adversity mattered because we would face it together. Having a loving teammate was the reason for the union. We surrendered to the idea of not knowing where we were going to live with both of our leases expiring in a matter of hours. We sat there, just appreciating this new life and all that was coming with it.

Minutes later, we got a call and we were approved for an apartment. Life began to take twists and turns as I got a job, we had a wedding, she got pregnant, we started to look for a house, and no matter what came our way, I thought about how it felt sitting in that Chick-Fil-A years ago accepting whatever was about to hit us.

It makes me thankful. And I continue to find rearview moments like that twin bed in my mother's house. Or my first car, the 1995 Lexus that I purchased in

2011 that got me around so much and was in decent shape. Before that, I was on the train and when I moved to Atlanta, my girl and I shared her vehicle. My rearview gratitude reminds me that the present is amazing. That is how I started to visualize the future and be happy about the present. When we lived in a ranch home in Stone Mountain, Georgia, we put up pictures of the homes we wanted to purchase. In less than a year, we ended up moving to a house worth more than the ones we had in the photographs. I wasn't upset about the Stone Mountain house I was in, I embraced it, I loved it, I was thrilled to be there daily and share the memories. We made that small space into a lovely, warm, comforting home where we began raising our first son, and the universe knew that.

And now we keep adding, like practicing mathematics,
The family is expanding,
Career moves we were planning,
Are coming into fruition,
By simply just understanding,
Got a bigger house and whip, and I promise that I'm not bragging,
The secret is...be joyful without it, then you attract it.

I wrote this when I got the news that I was having another son. We had just moved into our new house after staying with my wife's parents in an Atlanta apartment for over a month. Two adults and a three-year-old boy crammed in a room was uncomfortable, but everyday I was thankful that it wasn't a hotel that we had to pay for, or that we didn't have to sleep in a car, or with some friend that would've wanted to kick us out. We had family that had our best interest in mind as we looked for a house. We didn't expect ours to sell so fast and it left us stuck for some time. There were complications with the actual sale of our new home that delayed the move. But at no time was I bothered. When we finally moved in, more gratitude poured out, and to this day, I have pictures of home renovations and new vehicles taped up in my closet, I even have pictures of checks that I know will come to me. The key is to be ecstatic about where you are right now because it is truly a blessing. That is *The Secret.*

· · · · ·

Week 10 To-Do List: Write down ten things you would like to attract. You can list a vehicle, a job, a child, a home, an appliance, whatever you want to have in your possession is on its way to you. Now look at each item and picture yourself enjoying the drive, or relaxing on your deck, or chilling on the beach resort, just let the vibrations flow through you as you envision what it feels like to have what you know is coming to you. Feel free to do this every day or whenever you need to.

WEEK 11

THE RESOLUTION

You don't need motivational speakers,
Or someone's hatred to reach you,
Or doctors changing your features,
Even a sermon from the greatest of preachers,
Could be a waste if it's not with you all the days of the week,
It's making you weaker,
Don't wait...
For a better job, great boss,
Tax return, new love, bigger place, weight loss,
Mixtape is dropping; you swear it will get you popping,
Or as soon as your credit gets fixed, you're about to take off,
It's like waiting for Christmas to open presents,
When every day is a gift that was pre-sent, it's your presence,
On earth, believe you're worth more than money,
You're not a peasant,
You measure yourself by salaries, that can be why you're stressing,

Your New Year's Resolution is evolution,
Gym membership, that you never use,
Or the weight that you're never losing,
The growth is spiritual, when you're self-improving,
The answer's in the mirror, and yes it's proven,
The most expensive bed is your deathbed,
Even if you're paid,
It won't matter how much you've saved,
Once you lay down and you're on your way out, There's no amount of money
that would make someone trade,
Stop waiting to live

This is a still photo from my Bartalk video series that inspired this book. It feels like I'm really talking to myself in this shot so I used it as a reminder to stop waiting for a new year to make a resolution.

THE RESOLUTION

You don't need motivational speakers,
Or someone's hatred to reach you,
Or doctors changing your features,

I am not a motivational speaker. And even though some mornings I listen to them to start my day off with positive energy, the key word is "need." I use videos as reminders because some days are harder than others to stay in the light. Often, we feel like we need something or someone to push us. Just like the words from speakers are helpful, so is refusal, or disapproval, or some form of criticism to add fuel to your flame. I am consistently voicing my opinion that the best self-help process is to empower yourself so you don't need a book, a scripture, or a hater. There is a teacher in the mirror.

Even a sermon from the greatest of preachers,
Could be a waste if it's not with you all the days of the week,
It's making you weaker,

Speaking of scriptures, I used to go to church when I was searching for something. There was something special about being in a house of worship on a Sunday morning with everyone in there sharing the same thirst for positive light. It was a beautiful experience as an adult. The shorter services, the passionate sermons that didn't just preach Bible verses, there were teachings, morals, and jewels that I could apply to life.

One day, I decided that I had received everything I needed from the church experience. I no longer needed the spiritual refill every week. For some reason, I had consumed enough sermons, words, and lessons that I could call on them and perform Samaritan actions at any time. I no longer needed to hear the choir to feel goodness in my soul. I didn't have to dress up, prepare myself mentally, or be around others who were on the same path. I had it. I will expand on this later, but if you're still trying to get to the point I'm speaking of, it's fine. Some of us just don't know that there can be a goal. There's nothing wrong with wearing glasses for your sight, a cane to help you walk, or makeup to cover a blemish. But glasses come off, the cane can be put down, and makeup wipes away. Strengthen your weakness, especially if it's your faith in a higher power and ultimately, yourself.

Don't wait...
For a better job, great boss,
Tax return, new love, bigger place, weight loss,
Mixtape is dropping; you swear it will get you popping,
Or as soon as your credit gets fixed, you're about to take off,
It's like waiting for <u>Christmas</u> to open <u>presents,</u>
When every day is a <u>gift</u> that was <u>pre-sent</u>, it's your presence,
On earth, believe you're worth more than money,
You're not a peasant,
You measure yourself by salaries, that can be why you're stressing,

We all have dates circled on our calendar that relate to some type of change, future happiness, or relief. I look forward to breaks from work and tax refunds. I'm excited about Saturday every week because I get to spend more time with my family. But none of those dates and times that I anticipate can subtract any joy from this moment right here. As much as I desire this book to be in your hands, or this audio to feed your soul, I take just as much pleasure in crafting every word. That is the key to being in the moment. You must find some good in the space you are in, no matter how much another moment in time seems more desirable.

Your New Year's Resolution is evolution,
Gym membership, that you never use,
Or the weight that you're never losing,
The growth is spiritual, when you're self-improving,
The answer's in the mirror, and yes it's proven,

We all get caught up in New Year's Resolutions and the weight-loss pledges and whatever else we decide to take on to make ourselves feel like we're improving.

Before doing any of that physical work, ask yourself what would you really like to change about you and why. Don't just start changing eating habits and going to the gym for one month. Dig deep. The answer is within you and you can find the fuel to make whatever life alteration you need. If it's time for change, there won't be much internal pushback. Your mind and body will align to shift your daily moves and through that, you'll see how you can give up eating a certain type of food or you can add a regimen to your day. Please do not be hard on yourself if you relapse or start and stop a pledge that you made. Be confident that you will be alerted when it's time to make a change. And then you will.

The most expensive bed is your deathbed,
Even if you're paid,
It won't matter how much you've saved,
Once you lay down and you're on your way out,
There's no amount of money that would make someone trade,
Stop waiting to live

To sum this up, once again, the time and money correlation comes into play as I touch on what it's like to be close to the end of life. Can you imagine what people who experience terminal illness feel as the end approaches? You probably can't think that far because it's a morbid and scary thought. The point I'm making is that the only thing anyone would pray for is time. They would want more time with loved ones, more time to experience joy, and more time to live.

· · · · ·

Week 11 To-Do List: If you can remember your last five New Year's Resolutions, write them down. How did you do with each one? Do you remember them? How long were you committed to the resolutions? Compare each resolution and take a look at how much you've grown over the years and start to think about the approaching New Year and what you might want to add.

WEEK 12

THE PROCRASTINATOR

I'm trying to get this paper right,
I need to get my life straight,
I'm on my way to get a hotter car, and some new gear, and a nice place,
I'm about to start this regimen,
I gotta see myself at the right weight,
Next week for real, I'm in the gym,
I need a six-pack, and a tight shape,
I should look for a better job, but I probably need to get more degrees,
And with more degrees, that'll make me hot,
I want to find someone to love me for me,
I just babysit, in these relationships, that don't work out; then I'm forced to leave,
I want to stop lying,
See time's flying, one day I'll wake and be fifty-three,
Or sixty-one, with a son, that I keep telling what I could have been,
If I focused more, that would've opened doors, Yo this is God's fault, the place
He put me in,

I need to place the blame, because that'll make me sane,
Instead of making change, it's hard to look within,
I keep talking about the stuff I need to do,
And how to make these moves or when I should begin,
High school, I didn't make the team, I kept trying out,
Grown man, you know I had to take the word "trying" out,
Of my vocab, it got so bad, that being unsung was all I cried about,
I was lost, but I'm finally found,
You can't stand for something when you're lying down so good morning

My graduation day from Delaware State University in 1999 with my best man Ian Heyward and my former roommate and rap partner Dennis Quallo. I learned how to battle procrastination in college, sometimes I win the battle.

THE PROCRASTINATOR

I'm trying to get this paper right,
I need to get my life straight,
I'm on my way to get a hotter car, and some new gear, and a nice place,
I'm about to start this regimen,
I gotta see myself at the right weight,
Next week for real, I'm in the gym,
I need a six-pack, and a tight shape,

Procrastination is typical for most of us. It starts with the intention to improve one's self or complete a necessary task. Similar to what happens when we make resolutions, we tend to put them off because it's easier to make an excuse for why we're not exercising, or why we haven't worked on the project that was marked on our calendar. When you become a chronic procrastinator, you begin to invent reasons for deferring, delaying, and putting off until tomorrow.

Some people procrastinate because they need the pressure of time and a near deadline to create focus. Others procrastinate because there is no consequence or penalty for delaying the initiation or completion of something. I was someone who put off any task that I knew would bring me discomfort. Once I was able to pinpoint that I may not want to put together a table because the directions might be unclear and I would feel defeated if I couldn't figure it out helped me identify my true reason for procrastinating. I consistently desire being good at any endeavor I embark on. Sometimes, if I know I will be challenged, I delay the process.

Some of us are stuck with a "fixed mindset" and we believe that the talents, gifts, and intelligence we possess are all inherited. I had to adopt a "growth mindset" where I viewed challenges and pitfalls as springboards for escalation. Before I transitioned to this new mindset, I was convinced that I wasn't handy, I wasn't good at math, and I had an "imposter syndrome" when it came to being a writer. Find your reason for procrastination.

I should look for a better job, but I probably need to get more degrees,
And with more degrees, that'll make me hot,

The job/school cycle is a very real option for most adults. Continuing education can increase earnings and debt simultaneously. The decision becomes just as difficult as actual classes. To consider dedicating time to become a student just so you can potentially make more money seems logical in some ways, but advancing in a career is about experience, not necessarily a piece of paper that shows that you literally invested in yourself.

These bars are more about the reason why you haven't made a move that you decided was best for you. If you believe education is the path but fear of failure or the unknown is holding you back, then procrastination is rearing its annoying head in your life.

I want to find someone to love me for me,
I just babysit, in these relationships, that don't work out; then I'm forced to leave,
I want to stop lying,
See time's flying, one day I'll wake and be fifty-three,
Or sixty-one, with a son, that I keep telling what I could have been,
If I focused more, that would've opened doors, Yo this is God's fault, the place He put me in,

It's easy to say we want to find someone special and it's common to find ourselves in situations that we know are not the best. I wrote this to place myself inside the mind of a procrastinator that felt like at some point in his future, he would wake up talking about his past life as if it were not his fault.

The present is a pre-sent moment that is truthfully all there is on the timeline. Everything else is a figment of your imagination. We continuously recreate present moments over and over again but it is not the easiest task to be "in the moment."

When I was in college, my minor was Theatrical Arts and I took a Play Production course in my senior year. My professor was the late, great Dr. Kenyatta. Our final assignment was to write short plays and have our classmates act in them. I was an actor in a short play that one of my classmates wrote and my character was having a conflict with his girlfriend in the screenplay. The scene was set at my character's home and during the rehearsal; I took off my shoes and paraded around the stage in my socks because Dr. Kenyatta suggested that I wouldn't be in my house wearing shoes. In one of our rehearsals on the stage, my sock got caught on a nail and I physically stumbled, and then I lost my line and broke character. I apologized and asked everyone to reset. Dr. Kenyatta pulled me to the side and told me that if my sock got caught on a nail, then my character's sock got caught on a nail. He told me there was no reason to leave the scene for anything less than a gunshot. He gave me the idea that once I was in the moment; it was up to me to stay there. I never forgot that lesson. I used it in the recording booth when I rapped, I used it on stage when I performed, and I used it in class when it was time to pay attention. I will always remember the hole in my sock that caused me to stay in the moment. By the way, after that I wore slippers for every rehearsal and the actual show.

I need to place the blame, because that'll make me sane,
Instead of making change, it's hard to look within,
I keep talking about the stuff I need to do,
And how to make these moves or when I should begin,

This mindset is common; looking within can be truly painful and unsettling. I can recall times when I thought about being a teacher. I kept researching the steps to do it, and every time I got more information, it would slow me down because it seemed overwhelming.

There's not much else to say about procrastination except that you have the power to stop it. I've asked you to analyze why you defer, I've given you tips to approach your bad habits, and I've offered pieces of my story that haunted me and caused me to fear uncertainty and pushed me to hide shame. How does one go from being a person with terrible follow-through to someone that can see a process through from beginning to end with diligence and detail? The answer to the riddle is to take everything in incremented, small steps. If you know that paying a certain bill slips your mind, make sure you set up auto-pay for it (if possible). If you're in school and you have a project or paper due in 40 days, make a new habit to always start working on a part of it right away, then set a schedule to go back to it. Gradually create new habits and do not define yourself as a procrastinator. Stop.

High school, I didn't make the team, I kept trying out,
Grown man, you know I had to take the word "trying" out,
Of my vocab, it got so bad, that being unsung was all I cried about,
I was lost, but I'm finally found,
You can't stand for something when you're lying down so good morning

The story that I will tell my sons when they ask about trying out for a team is the one where I got cut from the eighth grade basketball team. I had just started playing basketball the year prior and I was horrible. I was also around 5'6" and slim. I only wanted to make the team because all the popular boys were on the team. I wanted to be a part of their brotherhood.

When I got cut, I didn't accept it. I went right to Coach Davis and told him I needed to be a part of the squad somehow. I remember standing in his office and looking at him with a cold stare. I wasn't going to leave without another opportunity. I wanted to be one of the cool kids. He let me try out again at a different position and I made the team. One year after that, I went to Brooklyn Technical High School with hopes to make the JV squad. I was around 5'8" with very little knack for the game but I loved to play. Tryouts were a nightmare. I got ripped (the ball stolen) bringing the ball up the court multiple times. If there was a freshmen team, I could've easily made it, but Tech didn't have one, and JV had super sophomores like Solomon Abel and my future manager Kevin Johnson who should have been on the varsity team. I sucked and I got cut. Ironically, the JV coach Darryl Rock and Coach Davis were friends, so my reluctance to wear my middle school jersey worked against me. Not that it would have mattered anyway. The point of the story is that I didn't learn from one year prior when I didn't take no for an answer. The teacher in the mirror was right there begging me to learn from my own moves but I didn't heed the lesson.

Or maybe I didn't feel like I deserved to be a part of the team so I used it as fuel. After that, I stopped believing in tryouts. If I wanted to make a team, I did whatever it took to make that team. If I wasn't good enough to make it, I accepted that, but I wasn't going to try to do anything. That wasn't my last time being cut from something. But it was my last time feeling like I should've done more. You cannot stand for something when you're lying down.

· · · · ·

Week 12 To-Do List: List all the tasks that you have to do that you've put off for more than one week. It could be cleaning a closet, dusting furniture, writing a script, or calling a friend. I want you to attack the smallest, easiest task and make that the goal for the week. My goal is to make my bed every day for one week. If you don't make your bed daily, start there. Form new habits slowly.

WEEK 13

THE LESSON

Your salary isn't your soul,
Who you are, is not your profession,
Degrees do not define you,
Your worth is not your possessions,
Employers are not your bosses,
Your pockets are not reflections
Of everything you're intended to be when you reach potential,
Joy is your true intention,
Surpasses any invention,
Or "like," or "comment," or "mention,"
Your job is just an extension,
So what you accumulate doesn't make your entire essence,
The place you live, what you drive, what you wear, and what you're digesting,
The oxygen you inhale every hour, minute, and second,
Is God giving you breath and my message before your death,
Is to live like there's a limit on moments that you have left,
The formality of mortality's something hard to accept,
When my bank account <u>lessened</u>, I stressed, but I learned some <u>lessons,</u>
Obsessing over regrets is the recipe for regression,
So this is more like confession, to press against your oppression,
I was counting my accounts; I wasn't counting my blessings,
Your attitude can get messy from having too much dissension,
But if you add gratitude what that'll do,
Is raise your latitude, you'll gain altitude,
And feel glad to see that ascension,
Me?
I used to stress about the date my bills were <u>due by,</u>
Now I'm planning family trips to visit <u>Dubai,</u>
So every time a <u>plane comes,</u> it's hard to <u>complain,</u>
I celebrate whether sun or rain, no matter what happens

The cover for my 2012 EP entitled *The 9.2.5*. Each song was an ode to the employee life that I feared when I was a youngster. I did an EP every month that year, which was a part-time job.

THE LESSON

Your salary isn't your soul,
Who you are, is not your profession,
Degrees do not define you,
Your worth is not your possessions,
Employers are not your bosses,
Your pockets are not reflections
Of everything you're intended to be when you reach potential,
Joy is your true intention,
Surpasses any invention,
Or "like," or "comment," or "mention,"
Your job is just an extension,
So what you accumulate doesn't make your entire essence,
The place you live, what you drive, what you wear, and what you're digesting,

Although I spent multiple bars running down everything that does not define the core of your being, you may be wondering what part of you delineates your nature. Your character can be loosely described by a few factors. One of them is how you make people feel, another is what people say about you when you're not around, and lastly, there is how you treat others that cannot benefit you in any way.

Our lives are often consumed with our jobs, our supervisors, our funds, our social media posts, and all the extensions of us that represent our lifestyle.

So what is the lesson? The lesson is all about the impression. The mark you leave behind when others mention you. Even if they talk about your talent, your house, or the car you drive, your goal is to express and exhibit the highest vibration and version of yourself and receive that energy in return.

The oxygen you inhale every hour, minute, and second,
Is God giving you breath and my message before your death,
Is to live like there's a limit on moments that you have left,
The formality of mortality's something hard to accept,

Jay-Z once said that the only thing worse than getting old is not getting old. I remember internalizing those lyrics when I was a college student. Every birthday was a reminder that I gained more wisdom, had more experience, and I was learning more about myself.

Sheek Louch rapped a similar lyric that boasted, "Keep hunger/and plan for the future 'cause you figure/you gon' be older, way longer than you gon' be younger" on "Money, Power, Respect." Rap was not just entertainment to me, I used insightful rap lyrics as poetic quotes to guide my daily moves. As much as I tried to remind myself that getting old was a good thing, Sheek's words reminded me that youth was temporary. Once I graduated from college I kept thinking that I would never be younger than I am today. During my twenties, I felt my youth slipping away so much that I didn't enjoy the decade at all. I remember being 24 years old and feeling ancient because I hadn't accomplished anything I set out to do. There's a difference between cherishing moments and living life to the fullest and being paranoid about dying so much that you can't relish the present.

When my bank account lessened, I stressed, but I learned some lessons,
Obsessing over regrets is the recipe for regression,

Success is not only different for each person but it varies according to your age and stage of your life.

For me, I wanted to have my own apartment, my own car, and enough financial freedom to go out and eat without worrying about the bill. But it's easy to concern yourself with what you want without looking at what you have.

Losing my record deal was one of the scariest times of my life. My ego was bruised and I was concerned with how my peers and fans would view me. Was I a failure? I had so many regrets and thoughts about what I should've done differently. I could not move forward for years. I was consumed with my story. I wrote about it, I rapped about it, I talked about it. I complained about it as if someone would come in and magically fix everything. Even when I tried to be positive, I was still scorned and confused. I didn't know why my path was so difficult. My social life was on hold for my career and I had missed out on so much joy. I needed to find peace.

I don't know if you have a missed opportunity in your life that you go back to often in your mind. Some of us have "almost" moments or moves that would have changed the course of our journeys and dwelling on them can only cause heartache. Now when I think about what would've panned out differently if I had turned right instead of left, I imagine life without my family and I am instantly jolted back to reality.

So this is more like confession, to press against your oppression,
I was counting my accounts, I wasn't counting my blessings,

I had done everything in my adult life within my power to avoid a job with a set salary. I didn't want someone to tell me what my output was worth before I completed the work. It didn't matter how much the salary was going to be, I always envisioned being able to work for what I earned and receiving the direct payment right away. So the first time I was presented with a small salary after my rap career took a halt, I was surprisingly excited. It was refreshing to know when my next check was coming and what I could do with it. I had been issued checks as a rap artist that were worth triple what I was making per year as an educator, but I was in a place where the salary didn't define me. Teachers, administrators, and principals that looked at me like I was at the bottom of the educational totem pole didn't bother me. I was worth more than they could imagine.

Your attitude can get messy from having too much dissension,
But if you add gratitude what that'll do,
Is raise your latitude, you'll gain altitude,
And feel glad to see that ascension,
Me?
I used to stress about the date my bills were due by,
Now I'm planning family trips to visit Dubai,

So every time a <u>plane comes</u>, it's hard to <u>complain,</u>
I celebrate whether sun or rain, no matter what happens

I am going to go more into depth about the origin of the lesson I learned involving the act of being thankful in a later chapter. For now, I want to focus on one aspect of the magical power of gratitude, and that is the monthly recurring dues tied to utilities, activities, luxuries, and necessities. Most people refer to these cyclical charges as bills.

There was a time when opening a bill would frighten me. Once companies began using paperless bills, the emails with the startling number in bold print would give me the shakes. It didn't matter what kind of bill it was, whether it was a phone bill, power bill, gas bill, or cable bill, I opened the email with paralyzing fear most of the time because I didn't want to see a number that would cripple my account.

I graduated from college in 1999. I received financial aid in the form of student loans that I needed to pay back once I was awarded my degree. I did not pay the lender, Sallie Mae, a dime for over a decade. In 2012, I was focused on becoming a real grownup that would one day hope to be a husband and father, and I felt like it would be a good idea to look at my credit score. My score was pretty terrible but more importantly, I began to answer the calls from creditors. One of those creditors was collecting on behalf of my student loan and the amount was around $40,000. The representative talked to me for some time and she shared her experience with paying back her college loans and how she tied the payments to all the knowledge she obtained and the fun she had. It may have been a tactic to get me to commit to a payment plan, but she was very open about attending an HBCU and pledging Zeta and she probably offered too much information on a business call, but it worked. She mentioned that her time at school was priceless and whatever monthly bill she had negotiated with the federal loan company was reasonable enough to pay. I wish I could remember that young woman's name but she changed my life and altered my view of paying back loan installments. She was right that there was no price that can quantify what I learned, the friends I made, and the memories that I shared with schoolmates. She convinced me to enroll in a 9-month payment plan that would scrub some of the bad reports off my credit as long as I paid the monthly bill on time. I paid the bill every month for 13 months and once I was done, my credit score went up and I was in good standing with the lender.

Since then, I stopped looking at bills as horrific reminders that I needed to spend money on something that wasn't necessarily tangible. I felt fortunate to be able to afford cable. I was lucky that I had enough money in my account to live somewhere and to drive a car. I saw my ability to keep my lights on and use the Internet as a blessing. Bills are no longer the enemy.

· · · · ·

Week 13 To-Do List: Write down the bill that bothers you the most. It could be a high interest rate on your mortgage or a car note that is too much. Are the rewards from the product or service equivalent to the amount you pay? If not, what amount would be fair? If so, try to change the way you view the bill. Be happy that you get to have access to a service and all you pay is a fee.

WEEK 14

THE FATHER HOOD

Back in the days, I had a rap line saying I would never be a father,

That was fear and just feeling inadequate,

And plus I couldn't dream I'd find a queen that I would want to be my partner,

Especially one that didn't already have a kid,

I wanted us both to feel clueless and novice, ignorant, foolish,

Not a baby-mother, slip-up, or accident,

I wanted to gaze at a little human,

And think what am I doing?

Asking God do I deserve all this happiness?

In 2001, Beanie Sigel spit about it,

And I couldn't relate,

I was trying to get rich and be great,

The way he broke it down though, I couldn't wait,

He said, "I can't explain it when I pick up my sons, and look at my face,"

And now I'm like a planet with a couple of suns,

And the shine is so surreal, I look at what I've become,

I went from me, myself, and I, being selfish and young,

To a provider, rider, idol, and protector in one,

And if you ask me to describe it, or try and give you a vibe of what it felt like at the moment my child took his first cry,

Or to give you words now,

That would somewhat summarize,

The emotions that I go through,

With two sets of tiny eyes,

Staring at me with the world in their palms,

I'm guiding their lives,

I am stuck,

All I can tell you is there is no greater high,

It's the apex of a vision that seemed evasive,

It's the pinnacle of wealth that supersedes any paper,

It's realizing your whole life,

That you were just an <u>amateur</u> but managed to find someone amazing to <u>procreate</u> with,

A lot of amateurs are procreating,

Sperm donor, Rolling Stones, that just walked away,

But I want to celebrate the superheroes, first male role models,

Dads and stepdads,

Happy Father's Day

Meet Cairo K. Williams and Zaire K. Williams. You can see why I wake up thankful each day.

THE FATHER HOOD

Back in the days, I had a rap line saying I would never be a father,
That was fear and just feeling inadequate,

The rap line that I had many years ago on a song called "Sad and Lonely" mentioned something about me not wanting to plant a seed but I honestly can't remember the motivation for writing it. I can remember that for the early part of my twenties, I wanted to outlast all of my friends as the eternal bachelor with no kids. I was driven solely by my career and I didn't want anyone to throw me off my mission. Also, there was the glaring issue of finances that always loomed around in my head. How could I take care of a child without a high-paying job, my own place, and a partner that I loved?

And plus I couldn't dream I'd find a queen that I would want to be my partner,
Especially one that didn't already have a kid,
I wanted us both to feel clueless and novice, ignorant, foolish,
Not a baby-mother, slip-up, or accident,
I wanted to gaze at a little human,
And think what am I doing?
Asking God do I deserve all this happiness?

I need to address the part about being a stepparent. I don't want to offend anyone that made the decision to adopt a child that they didn't contribute genetics to. I believe stepping in as a parent is one of the noblest acts any person can do. My wife and I are both products of homes where the bloodlines were not consistently connected to everyone in the household. That could be part of why I always wanted to create children after marriage.

There are many moving parts that I considered back when being a stepdad was a possibility. I've always felt as though there were at least four families involved in a child's life when one of their parents is not related to them by blood.

1. The first family is connected to the mother of the child. Grandparents, best friends, cousins, and everyone related to the mother will probably have the most contact with the kid.

2. Then there's the biological father. If I were dating someone and her kid had to spend time with the man that created them, that means that his family also has some contact, and possibly influence, on the youngster. And when that kid is in that space, I would have very little ability to protect or weigh-in on anything.

3. If that same father decides to have another relationship, when he's with that woman, she may feel as if the child is a part of her family. If he dates multiple women, then that adds more factors, but for argument's sake, if he has one woman, her family will be involved in that child's life.

4. And then there's the hypothetical stepdad. Assuming I'm in this imaginary role, my thought process was always that I would have to love the child and mother enough to endure the strenuous, complicated, but beautiful union. That means that my family would embrace my new youngster as if I produced the kid from my loins.

So that's my rant. I said all of that to say I really wanted to have the experience I'm having right now where my wife and I are learning how to raise these boys together, all of our kids are under one roof, and we all have the same last name.

It may sound like a "happily ever after" life but there is no blueprint for raising a magnificent family, and every day there are challenges and triumphs. There are also various ingredients and recipes for the family of your dreams. You do not need to have all of your kids in the same house or coming from the same parents to have a wonderful familial experience. In the words of the great Will Smith, child raising is more of an art than it is a science.

In 2001, Beanie Sigel spit about it,
And I couldn't relate,
I was trying to get rich and be great,

The way he broke it down though, I couldn't wait,
He said, "I can't explain it when I pick up my sons, and look at my face,"
And now I'm like a planet with a couple of suns,
And the shine is so surreal, I look at what I've become,
I went from me, myself, and I, being selfish and young,
To a provider, rider, idol, and protector in one,

When I heard Beanie Sigel's line from the song "Nothing Like It," I was in a space where I couldn't see myself as a father or even a boyfriend. But the depth of his line resonated with me. It put weight on the moment he first met his son and I can safely say, he added gravity to parenthood for me. I was a witness to many of my peers and associates creating humans and hardly valuing the experience. I had friends who had children that they didn't get to see often, and it made me feel as if they didn't grasp what it meant to really raise a person.

But Beanie was fully aware of how serious the role of parenting is. I had the sumptuous moments of holding my sons at birth and feeling exactly what Beans talked about. I religiously sit and marvel at the fact that these young boys are here and that they chose me to be a part of their world. It is honestly overwhelming.

And if you ask me to describe it, or try and give you a vibe of what it felt like at the
moment my child took his first cry,
Or to give you words now,
That would somewhat summarize,
The emotions that I go through,
With two sets of tiny eyes,
Staring at me with the world in their palms,
I'm guiding their lives,
I am stuck,
All I can tell you is there is no greater high,

If you have a child then you know that words don't really describe what it feels like to bring offspring into the world. If you don't, then the most I can explain about the experience is the confusion that I felt when my son was born.

I was confused because I was under the impression that love had a limit. I was watching my wife during the Cesarean section surgery and the whole time, I kept my eyes on her. I was only concerned about her safety and ease while my son was being freed from her womb. She was my priority. Of course I was concerned about him making the transition but at that point, my view of love had a salary cap on it. When I held him in my arms after he stopped wailing for what seemed like 30 minutes, my heart metaphorically grew. I could feel my ego and fear withering away and a pair of angel wings growing to shield over my family. It was a surreal moment that I can probably sum up by explaining the ride home where I drove with both hands on the steering wheel, the radio off, and I probably changed lanes once while going way under the speed limit. I was a changed man forever on September 11th, 2015.

And what might seem crazier is that after having a boy, I was praying for a little girl when my wife told me she was pregnant again. Once again, I was skeptical about the power of love. I was so enthralled with my guy Zaire that I couldn't imagine having another boy that I would compare and contrast constantly, and there was no way another boy could live up to the standards set by my firstborn. I thought that in order for me to love another child of mine in the way that was fitting, that child would have to be a little girl version of my wife. Silly me, I had no idea my heart could again expand in a way that seemed abnormal. On April 11th, 2019, Cairo was born and once again, love broke through the boundaries I thought were in place. I don't have a favorite son and I'm not happier when one is around and the other isn't. My love for these three people is something that I can't compute or quantify because I was unaware that it existed. What's even funnier is that I still doubt that the love for them can increase. And the more it increases, the more I embrace the fact that love is powerful and limitless. I hope that helps.

It's the apex of a vision that seemed evasive,
It's the pinnacle of wealth that supersedes any paper,
It's realizing your whole life,
That you were just an _amateur_ *but managed to find someone amazing to* _procreate_
with,

A lot of amateurs are procreating,
Sperm donor, Rolling Stones, that just walked away,
But I want to celebrate the superheroes, first male role models,
Dads and stepdads,
Happy Father's Day

I never liked the term "Deadbeat Dad." I salute any clever alliteration, but the term suggests that a man had a child and is completely absent from the child's life. There are an infinite number of scenarios that keep fathers from raising their children. Unfortunately, men are frequently judged harshly for not taking an active role in raising a child that they created. And maybe they should be in most cases. I do believe that once you do the deed that produces a human, those two people have a responsibility to conjure an atmosphere that is conducive to the young child's growth and development.

We know that every couple that makes a baby is not meant to be together forever. That is why I wanted to focus on the dads that show up daily to ensure that their kid is excelling in life. So whether you're a stepdad, a biological father, a super-active uncle, or you had a father that was present, I want you to think about how the role of the paternal parent shapes our society. If you had one or didn't, how did that affect you and your view of the world? I know growing up with a loving mother as the head of the household and a father who worked so much that I barely saw him made me want my home structure as an adult to be different. More importantly, I wanted to be more than a working dad or a provider dad. I want my kids to look at me and see their first male role model, a real life modern-day superhero.

• • • • •

Week 14 To-Do List: Who was the first television dad that showed you what it meant to be a great father? How did your dad or single mom measure up to the dad on the small screen? Write about it and read it. Does it help you understand your view of parenthood and why you move the way you do?

WEEK 15

THE QUEEN WITHIN

Before you judge that woman and recognize her flaws,
And all her shortcomings and who's she's been with before,
That's somebody's daughter thirst trapping, yeah it happens, but she probably
wasn't given the tools, so she looks lost,
When she was young and spoke proper,
They called her bourgeois instead of classy,
And then when she got loud they said ghetto instead of sassy,
Her hair was thick and lovely, tightly curled, they called it nappy,
And told her she was soft when being thoughtful made her happy,
Her dad gave his support, because he was ordered by the court,
Once a month the visits made her smile, but they were short,
So her idea of love was temporary, somewhat forced,
Because her mother blamed and shamed her counterpart for their divorce,
Then the adolescent years, the mirror caused deception,
The beauty others saw she couldn't find in her reflection,
People said, "Watch your weight," so then the pounds became obsession,
Girls were throwing hate so that inflamed her imperfections,
Boys were throwing praise and tried to mask it as affection,
Just to show off their erections,
And she tried to toss deflections,
But the absence of assurance, self-esteem, and true attention,
Made her seek a weak connection though she felt their real intentions,
She stopped the college classes 'cause she couldn't pay the price,
But her lashes always popped and her weave was staying tight,
Now she's older and she's scrolling on her phone all day and night,
Realizing if she shows some skin, she starts to gain some "likes,"
So the bread that was tuition, room and board, and paid for books,
It got used to slim her waist, lift her butt, and change her looks,

It's not her fault she doesn't know she's not a <u>pawn</u>, she's not a <u>rook</u>,

Since she was born, she's been a <u>queen</u>,

When people see that, they get shook,

So they want her insecure,

They want her waking up dependent,

On their products, on external factors that have been presented,

Just to tear her down, make her hurt, they won't tell her love,

Is being vulnerable AND powerful, 'cause that would build her up,

They don't want her well and healthy,

They want her to take <u>shortcuts</u>,

I want her to embrace her heritage, if it's a <u>short cut</u>,

Locks, braids, none of it matters, because when she shows up,

Her internal energy, speaks to us instantly,

So please, if you meet her and her royalty doesn't show,

Don't hold it against her, give her some time to grow,

Maybe she heard the B-word so much in her own house, maybe someone called her ugly and always made her feel low,

Maybe she's in one of those emotionally abusive relationships, and nobody told her it's time to go,

Because we lose direction, it doesn't mean we're lost,

Her beauty still comes across but maybe she doesn't know

L to R. Trenise, Tonnay, Tamera, and Dyamond surprised me with lunch for my birthday in 2019. These young queens were my seniors during my inaugural year as a Grad Coach at Carver High School in 2016. They changed my life by choosing me as a mentor. I always remind them that they are royalty and they remind me that I'm old.

THE QUEEN WITHIN

Before you judge that woman and recognize her flaws,
And all her shortcomings and who's she's been with before,
That's somebody's daughter thirst trapping, yeah it happens, but she probably wasn't
given the tools, so she looks lost,

What is a thirst trap? It's a term for posting pictures or videos of one's self that are meant to gain attention based on some type of physical attribute. We've all posted media of ourselves that we want people to acknowledge. I don't think there's anything wrong with starting a modeling career from the comfort of your home and nowadays women can make a living posting pictures of themselves in skimpy clothing exposing their curves. Some of them have pages dedicated to showing skin, and others use dance moves and sexual suggestions to gain followers and dollars.

I am guilty of following women that post seductive pictures on social media but I also become saddened by their posts. It's a conflicting place to be in because I am a father and I instantly think about the fact that these women are daughters of someone. No matter how much money they could possibly make, if I helped raise a girl that became a social media model full-time, I would probably feel a bit of shame because I would want her body to be a precious commodity that should not be viewed by the world.

But are my feelings warranted? Do I truly know the story behind every curvy, half-naked woman on Instagram? Am I aware of the ends that may justify her means? The answer is no. What makes the woman who shows her body different from the rapper that promotes violence? If they both generate income to feed families and use their voices to positively impact others, where does the judgment truly come from? Maybe it's a chauvinistic view that causes us to feel that because a woman has chosen to display her physique, that she is "lost."

When she was young and spoke proper,
They called her bourgeois instead of classy,

And then when she got loud they said ghetto instead of sassy,
Her hair was thick and lovely, tightly curled, they called it nappy,
And told her she was soft when being thoughtful made her happy,

This is a random rundown of possible history that may or not relate to anyone. What I want you to understand about these few bars is that negative connotations can shape young minds. If I never learned the word "nappy" and I was told my hair was beautiful growing up, would I have ever tried to put an S-Curl activator in my hair to look like Michael Jackson? Maybe Michael might not have needed those curls either.

During the 2019 school semester my friend and principal of Carver STEAM Academy Yusuf Muhammad organized an all-male assembly at the school. I asked one of my guys from the Respected Roots organization, Jaret Patterson, to come speak to the kids. I knew most of the young men in attendance and I asked them a question towards the end of the program. I wanted to know how many of them referred to the girls at the school as "bitches." Almost all of them raised their hands. Then I asked them if someone called their grandmother, mother, sister, or daughter a "bitch," what would they do. Most of them mumbled under their breath but the overall sentiment was that any person they cared about was not a "bitch" and they would be moved to violence if they had to defend the honor of a woman in their immediate family. What was the difference? I asked them if they were aware that the girls who went to school with them were daughters, granddaughters, and sisters of people who loved them. They knew that but they presented the fact to me that most of the girls didn't deserve respect. I informed them that there was a vicious cycle of negative connotations that they will always have the power to halt. Those types of conversations need to happen more often.

Her dad gave his support, because he was ordered by the court,
Once a month the visits made her smile, but they were short,
So her idea of love was temporary, somewhat forced,
Because her mother blamed and shamed her counterpart for their divorce,

The father is an integral piece of the family structure; his presence can set an example for generations while his absence can leave a gaping hole in growth and development for his seeds. Having a father is great, but if one parent vilifies the other, the family suffers. Hatred, distrust, dishonesty, and blame can become a part of a young person's psyche. If a kid has no idea that they had two parents that loved them equally because one parent poisoned the idea of the other, resentment can grow in the heart of the child. As much as I witnessed my own father play a huge role in leaving our household, my mother never made it seem like he was a bad person, nor did she blame him for their divorce. I understood that relationships change and so do the people that create the relationships.

Then the adolescent years, the mirror caused deception,
The beauty others saw she couldn't find in her reflection,
People said, "Watch your weight," so then the pounds became obsession,
Girls were throwing hate so that inflamed her imperfections,
Boys were throwing praise and tried to mask it as affection,
Just to show off their erections,
And she tried to toss deflections,
But the absence of assurance, self-esteem, and true attention,
Made her seek a weak connection though she felt their real intentions,

Beauty is the quality that gives pleasure or satisfaction to the senses of the beholder. When someone feels like they are not pleasing to the eyes, they search and seek approval in other ways. There are so many reasons people look for attention. The social media era puts the spotlight on "likes," "comments," and "followers." The key is to build up our adolescents so that the most frightening and mentally challenging phase of their lives has some solace and peace involved. Building them up comes with positive vocabulary to describe them, it means open conversations sans judgment, and it always speaks to the fact that well-balanced, careful choices are at the core of transitioning to adulthood.

I remember having a closed-door conversation with one of my students a few years ago, and she confessed to me that she was in an abusive relationship. I alerted the social worker but the young lady was not comfortable speaking to everyone about her situation. One morning, I noticed the sadness in her eyes, and the weight gain she tried to hide. I asked her to come talk to me when she had some free time and she did. The tears flowed and she divulged the fact that she was five months pregnant for her boyfriend. Although he stopped hitting her, he was still emotionally abusive. I wanted to be supportive without judging her so I asked her what she planned to do about her child on the way. She planned on keeping the child and raising the baby on her own. What stood out the most about our conversation was her reason for keeping the child. She said that she wanted someone that would finally love her unconditionally. I really didn't know what to say but I thought about her home life and some of the stories she told me, and then I could only sympathize with the feeling she spoke of. That talk with the young lady reminded me that there are factors at home that can gravely affect students' decisions and at that time, all I could do was support her and pray for the best.

She stopped the college classes 'cause she couldn't pay the price,
But her lashes always popped and her weave was staying tight,
Now she's older and she's scrolling on her phone all day and night,
Realizing if she shows some skin, she starts to gain some "likes,"
So the bread that was tuition, room and board, and paid for books,
It got used to slim her waist, lift her butt, and change her looks,
It's not her fault she doesn't know she's not a pawn, she's not a rook,
Since she was born, she's been a queen,
When people see that, they get shook,
So they want her insecure,
They want her waking up dependent,
On their products, on external factors that have been presented,
Just to tear her down, make her hurt, they won't tell her love,
Is being vulnerable AND powerful, 'cause that would build her up,
They don't want her well and healthy,
They want her to take shortcuts,
I want her to embrace her heritage, if it's a short cut,
Locks, braids, none of it matters, because when she shows up,

Her internal energy, speaks to us instantly,
So please, if you meet her and her royalty doesn't show,
Don't hold it against her, give her some time to grow,
Maybe she heard the B-word so much in her own house, maybe someone called her
ugly and always made her feel low,
Maybe she's in one of those emotionally abusive relationships, and nobody told her it's
time to go,
Because we lose direction, it doesn't mean we're lost,
Her beauty still comes across but maybe she doesn't know

This narrative is all about perspective. When I'm scrolling on Instagram and I see one of my former male students posing with guns or stacks of money, I am a bit disturbed because most times the kid has chosen to portray a role that isn't honest to his true self. Then I think about my high school days and how feeble I was. I avoided fights, I was nervous on the train as a freshman, and I was nowhere near the confident individual I turned out to be. Someone could have easily spotted me with a gun in my pants on a hip-hop DVD in 2003 and thought the exact same thing I thought about those youngsters. I am not in a position to judge anyone.

My role as a Graduation Coach affords me the opportunity to intervene when students are off-track when it comes to receiving a diploma on time. Every year I am invested in making sure my seniors cross the stage at the commencement ceremony. One particular year I can recall two female seniors that had lost faith and decided that graduation was not probable. I was instrumental in identifying the resolve within them, loading them up with online classes, and ultimately their determination to cross the academic finish line was admirable. I was proud that they made it.

That same year another young lady decided that school was not for her no matter how hard I pushed and advised, her mother was not on the same page with me about education. Years later I discovered through her acquaintances that she had not only become a mom but she was also working in a strip club as a dancer. That young queen is not a failure and she isn't necessarily misguided either. Her immediate family was always concerned with her earning money to assist the household. They were not focused on the young lady's empowerment through education. Sometimes I want to reach out to her but I am aware that my ego may be feeding me the idea that I can easily change someone's life for the better. There is a queen within her no matter what occupation she chooses.

Even if you haven't discovered the version of yourself that you are completely fond of, it doesn't mean you aren't royalty.

· · · · ·

Week 15 To-Do List: If there was one thing you could change about yourself, whether a physical or a characteristic trait, what would it be? Would you want to make your chest bigger, make your nose smaller, change your eye color, maybe become a little taller, take away some wrinkles, add length to your hair, or some inches to your backside, or make your gut disappear? Would you want to be more thoughtful, less egotistical, subtract some of your pettiness, or stop being negative? Imagine you altered that one aspect of your being. Would the physical change make you happier each day? Can you make the character switch right now?

Now take a look in the mirror and thank God for who you are. Whatever you thought about switching is not enough to delay the feeling of gratitude for this moment, for the beauty you possess, or for the individual you are. You are constantly improving and the process is ongoing, continue to grow in your own time.

WEEK 16

THE EXPERIENCE

I used to tell youngsters stay in school, dream big, beware of the drugs,
Respect life and learn to fight, instead of carrying slugs,
And strap up during sex because you're sharing your blood,
Like you're boxing and throwing punches without wearing a glove,
It doesn't matter if my message is endearing with love,
If all your peers can be thugs,
Until they appear for a judge,
That's why I stopped trying to reach 'em,
And I learned, don't preach, because words don't teach...
Experience does,
So you might have to drop out of school, have life get seriously real,
Get a low paying job, have some critical bills,
Catch an STD from a "Netflix and chill,"
Or make a baby with somebody that you don't really feel,
Or you start out with weed, but you're curious still,
So then prescriptions get filled, and you get addicted to pills,
Or you get in a confrontation that you could've walked away from,
Your toughness goes on display, and one of your peoples get killed,
Or your crew goes on a mission, and that illegal decision lands you in prison,
Now you've got some years to sit still,
With grown men giving orders and preparing your meals,
As a teenager, you shouldn't be preparing your will,
Got you thinking of all the knowledge that your parents had spilled,
Teachers, coaches, counselors, that tell you the deal,
But you ain't listen to the jewels that they shared and revealed,
So when you crash, just remember who was steering the wheel,
America's ill, especially if you're melanin-filled,
These cops will have you <u>catching bullets</u> like an <u>NFL drill,</u>

But these youngsters are hard to reach,
So I learned, don't preach,
Because when those words don't teach...
Experience will!

L to R. Arnardo Vargas Jr., Coach Williams, Darryl Parsons Jr., and Vinicius Viana at the North Springs High School Basketball Banquet in 2015. I used to train these young gentlemen before school and we are still bonded to this day.

THE EXPERIENCE

I used to tell youngsters stay in school, dream big, beware of the drugs,
Respect life and learn to fight, instead of carrying slugs,
And strap up during sex, because you're sharing your blood,
Like you're boxing and throwing punches without wearing a glove,

Working in the school system in Georgia, it has been a privilege to be a part of so many young lives. When it comes to mentoring and imparting wisdom, my method of communicating with them is always an even moderate tone.

I never encourage them to move too far right or left. I would never say, "Don't smoke." I would always say, "Don't let anything distract you from your end-game, don't let a substance become a habit, and be aware of the gateway to harder drugs out there." The key is not to make them feel like I'm an old man that never made mistakes. I want them to see me as an evolved version of them.

My message about sex is similar to the one I got from my health teacher during my sophomore year of high school. Mr. Yaged told me that 15 minutes is all it takes to ruin your whole life. The class reacted to the amount of time he chose to signify the length of a sexual act, but he was right. We were kids. We weren't having all-night sex sessions. And a lot of us were virgins. He showed us pictures of Syphilis and Gonorrhea symptoms in an attempt to inform us. He didn't try to scare us but he was laying out the facts. That is what I do. I present the facts.

It doesn't matter if my message is endearing with love,
If all your peers can be thugs,
Until they appear for a judge,
That's why I stopped trying to reach 'em,
And I learned, don't preach, because words don't teach...
Experience does,
So you might have to drop out of school, have life get seriously real,
Get a low paying job, have some critical bills,

Catch an STD from a "Netflix and chill,"
Or make a baby with somebody that you don't really feel,

The theme of this post is all about communicating messages to people who may not want to receive them. The receivers could be adults, young adults, or young teens, but the common thread is that when there is a preachy vibe attached to words of advice, even if they are extremely helpful, the listener tends to tune out.

I have seen plenty of students choose not to finish school and create babies before they were ready. And they almost always return to me years later expressing some form of regret. They never say, "I wish I didn't have this baby," or "I should've paid attention in school." But they do express that they made choices that weren't the best. And even though they had adults steering them in the right direction, they chose to instead learn from experience.

Or you start out with weed, but you're curious still,
So then prescriptions get filled, and you get addicted to pills,
Or you get in a confrontation, that you could've walked away from,
Your toughness goes on display, and one of your peoples get killed,

There's a movie that I promise to show my children when they're older, or my team if I ever decide to coach again. The film *Unguarded* is the story of former high school basketball star Chris Herren from Massachusetts who graduated in 1994. Chris was an exceptional guard with toughness and grit. Chris made it to the annual McDonald's High School Basketball All-American game with the top seniors in the nation.

He ended up going to Boston College, not far from his home.

Before his first game at BC, some women offered Chris, a kid who had never done any drugs, cocaine. They offered. He declined. They offered again. He declined again. There was no one there to stop him, advise him, give him some factual consequences, and maybe there was no health teacher that spat words that would seep in his subconscious like my own experience. After one more offer from the ladies, he accepted and did his first line of cocaine. His life changed forever.

The journey that Chris Herren explained throughout *Unguarded* is one of extreme despair, loss, deception, and what he describes as hitting rock bottom. Chris struggled with addiction for many years and it followed him to the NBA, to playing overseas, and beyond. It almost ruined his family and his relationship with his children and nearly took his life. I can't tell a young student that drinking "lean," popping pills, and smoking in excess will definitely lead to a dangerous path of addiction. There is no guarantee that any of that could happen. Marijuana is a pure plant that honestly does more healing than harm. But the feeling of being high and chasing highs can become elusive and critical.

Or your crew goes on a mission, and that illegal decision lands you in prison,
Now you've got some years to sit still,
With grown men giving orders, and preparing your meals,
As a teenager, you shouldn't be preparing your will,
Got you thinking of all the knowledge that your parents had spilled,
Teachers, coaches, counselors, that tell you the deal,
But you ain't listen to the jewels that they shared and revealed,
So when you crash, just remember who was steering the wheel,

The prison system is filled with men who made choices with someone else in mind. The action could have been a result of the girl that cheated, or needed someone to defend her honor. Maybe it was the dude that was making threats online, or it could be the easy score to move product from one city to another and just like that, life can change quickly. Young men can end up in one of the most respected and feared arenas, the prison system.

I had a partner in high school named Rob who was sort of a bad seed. He had a good heart but he was troubled in some ways and constantly getting into small confrontations. Back in the mid-90s, Rob borrowed his friend Junior's bicycle and didn't return it for days. Junior began to search for Rob and he made it known to their mutual acquaintances that he was upset. Junior made some threats that were exaggerated by others in the neighborhood. Since Rob heard that Junior was going to harm him when they saw each other, Rob prepared for violence.

Rob and Junior finally met up on a summer night in Brooklyn, New York. Rob felt as though the threats were disrespectful, and in his words, "Once I pulled it out, I had to use it." He shot his former friend a few times in the chest and went on the run for some days before turning himself in and serving 19 years in prison for premeditated murder. It's hard for Rob to identify with the anger he felt that day as a young teenager. He has turned his life around and is not looking back at his past. Rob spends a lot of his time speaking to high school students about the dangers of peer pressure, and the importance of mentorship and decision-making. Rob tells his story with the hopes that he reaches and alters the moves of troubled teens who could be on paths to destruction similar to him. There are young people out there that have the opportunity to change their direction before they become regretful adults. Words don't teach, but we still use them.

America's ill, especially if you're melanin-filled,
These cops will have you catching bullets like an NFL drill,
But these youngsters are hard to reach,
So I learned, don't preach,
Because when those words don't teach...
Experience will!

No matter what, we are all going to advise, assist, and add value to the lives of people that have not logged more years than us on the earth. It is much easier to present the pros and cons of decisions, share your past that may or may not mirror theirs, and most of all, let experience be their teacher. We must continue the work because for some students like myself, words may not teach but they sure can warn and stick with us.

· · · · ·

Week 16 To-Do List: If you are not a mentor or a mentee, who would you like to mentor? Mentoring is not about "saving" someone or raising them like you would raise your own offspring. Mentoring is about being a voice of reason, a listening ear, and using lessons from your own experiences to assist another person with their growth.

If you have someone guiding your decisions or you are the one on the coaching staff of someone's life, be more active in your role. Have some weekly check-ins because choices are all we have.

WEEK 17

THE D1 DREAM

I don't know who might need to hear this,

Daughter, nephew, cousin, or son,

A lot of youngsters are out here playing sports, and there's very few with a rare gift,

Either way, I pray you have fun,

Shout out to every coach, spending hours of your days every week, while no one sees what it takes to get it done,

And so many times I hear delusional students sounding so foolish, talking about they want to go Division One,

Oh you want to be a Blue Devil, Wildcat, Jayhawk, Seminole?

Hurricane, Hoya? The conversation's getting old,

How are you out here claiming that you want to be a Tarheel?

When you don't understand how going hard feels?

You don't love the process, or the journey on the court or on the field,

You're not practicing with a purpose,

Working out, improving skill,

You ain't training twice a day and maintaining stellar grades,

You don't cherish every sprint, every drill,

"Aye, aye, you! I'm talking to you,

The one sagging your pants off,

With no clue what AAU stands for,"

But that's where you're shining right?

And you average 23 without playing D, you just need Coach K to come and see,

Sure, let me chill, I will give you a little foresight

There's nothing wrong with playing *2K* and *Fortnite* all night,

But don't be an all-world gamer,

Then we see you in the game, you're just alright,

How about this?

Take the talent from that controller with your thumbs,

And when you say your team is weak,

Your school is lame, your coach is dumb,

You need to give yourself a hug, and hold the one and only person accountable,

For you not going Division One!

This picture was taken in 2014. When the head coach got ill, I had to take over as the North Springs Varsity Basketball Coach that night along with my partner and little bro Kendrick Reid. We lost to Riverwood. I'm still in touch with some of these young men. In an effort to teach them, I learned so much from them.

THE D1 DREAM

I don't know who might need to hear this,
Daughter, nephew, cousin, or son,
A lot of youngsters are out here playing sports, and there's very few with a rare gift,
Either way, I pray you have fun,
Shout out to every coach, spending hours of your days every week, while no one sees
what it takes to get it done,
And so many times I hear delusional students sounding so foolish, talking about they
want to go Division One,

One of the biggest issues I faced when I coached high school basketball was motivating the students that did not know what hard work looked like. Every year I was training or working with student-athletes that either did not value the classroom work as a part of their journey or felt like their efforts on the court were enough to land them an athletic scholarship.

They would start out as freshmen with lofty goals and high expectations. But once those students learned that their expectations had to be met with consistency and intense work ethic, they rarely chose the path that demanded sweat equity. There were no words I could speak to inform them that basketball was not something they loved, but it was a hobby and a way to express themselves and hang with friends.

When I was coaching high school basketball, I would offer my training services at 7 a.m. before school officially started for students that were serious about improving their games. One particular student named Brian was enthusiastic about me training him but he couldn't get to school early. He wanted me to train him after school and on the weekends. I was already coaching and I had a son on the way so I wasn't about to spend time with a student that wasn't truly dedicated. When I worked with youngsters in the mornings I would charge them one dollar, or I would ask them to buy me a chicken biscuit from Chick-Fil-A. Sometimes I would ask for five dollars and then I would return the money back to them after the session. I wanted them to feel like they were investing in themselves. Brian was different though because he made a lot of excuses and his performance on the court was nowhere near his potential. I proposed to him that I would work with him for 50 dollars per session. He was instantly upset that I was charging him but I assured him that there were other students who I was training at odd times and their parents had no issues paying for something they believed in. I let him know that I was not the only trainer who would be able to help him reach his goals but my time was valuable. He told me that his mother would not pay that price for a session and she wanted to know if I would do it for 25 dollars. I looked down at Brian's feet and saw brand new retro Jordans that were worth about $220. He knew exactly why I was looking down and he said, "These were a late birthday gift!" I guess he knew where I was going with my next statement. I told him that if he returned the expensive footwear and purchased some strength shoes, which were 120 dollars cheaper, I would train him for free. Brian and I never discussed basketball training again after that day.

As adults, we face the same issues. We believe we want something but when we find out what it entails to make it happen, we discover that we may have desires that outweigh what we thought we wanted.

Oh you want to be a Blue Devil, Wildcat, Jayhawk, Seminole?
Hurricane, Hoya? The conversation's getting old,
How are you out here claiming that you want to be a Tarheel?
When you don't understand how going hard feels?

A large percentage of the time that I ask young ballplayers what college they would like to attend, the answer is Duke. Sometimes I would get Kentucky or UNC, but for the most part, the Blue Devils are the landing spot for cool kids across the country. Duke creates pros and it has been a popular haven for top recruits looking to land in the NBA. To be recruited by Coach K, you need stellar grades, a killer work ethic, and a congenial attitude. But if you have no idea how to go hard, whose fault is that? If there is no one to tell you how to train, what to eat, and why your grades should be above average, then a child is left with nothing but an empty dream.

You don't love the process, or the journey on the court or on the field,
You're not practicing with a purpose,
Working out, improving skill,
You ain't training twice a day and maintaining stellar grades,
You don't cherish every sprint, every drill,

This part speaks to us all. Forget sprints and drills. Think about the drive to your job or the taxing thought of creating a business. The work, the attention to detail, the cost of equipment or licensing, or simply figuring out what you want your career to be can be tedious. And even more exhausting could be finding the time and mental energy to dedicate to an objective. The destination starts to seem far away or you accumulate resentment because it seems like others have it easier.

This is how plenty of students approach not just sports, but life. They are focused on results and the rewards and they forget about the process. How hard is it to fall in love with the work that leads to your aspiration? There is some joy in creating sweat equity. There is satisfaction in feeling physical pain for a cause. You don't want to just wake up and look in the mirror and see a fit physique. You want to work through every squat, crunch, and pound lifted to feel like you've earned every pound lost.

"Aye, aye, you! I'm talking to you,
The one sagging your pants off,
With no clue what AAU stands for,"
But that's where you're shining right?
And you average twenty-three without playing D, you just need Coach K to come and see,

The Amateur Athletic Union has been around for years. It has changed the landscape of high school, collegiate, and believe it or not, professional basketball. National tournaments provide exposure for students, adjust the individual rankings, and allow kids from all over to play with and against each other a lot earlier than years ago, when top players from across the country wouldn't see each other until they were in college.

What does AAU represent? It is a watered-down version of a basketball league that usually emphasizes winning at all costs. That means teamwork, defense, and molding talent are not the priorities when it comes to AAU. Kids with popular names get on teams together and dominate. Kids without notoriety find ways to make names for themselves playing for coaches that aren't going to speak to them about going to anyone's class, about working hard for a teacher, or possibly about playing the "right" way. It's a perfect route for a ball player that says, "I don't need to play for my school. I'll just play AAU." There's nothing wrong with that mindset until someone is recruiting the student and they ask the high school coach for a character trait. When a recruiter comes to watch a kid play in a high school game or an AAU league, they are viewing everything from body language on the bench, to interactions with teammates, to attentiveness in huddles. It is important to be valuable on the court, but it is equally important to be a treasured teammate and exhibit a coachable disposition.

Sure, let me chill, I will give you a little foresight...
There's nothing wrong with playing 2K *and* Fortnite *all night,*
But don't be an all-world gamer,
Then we see you in the game; you're just alright,
How about this?
Take the talent from that controller with your thumbs,
And when you say your team is weak, your school is lame; your coach is dumb,
You need to give yourself a hug, and hold the one and only person accountable,
For you not going Division One!

Like most of these lessons and messages, I am speaking to myself and the central focus is within. When I was a senior in high school, I didn't apply to any colleges because I was certain that I would receive a basketball scholarship. I was wrong. I had Division Three and Division Two schools beating down my door but as a 6'3" shooting guard who recognized his potential in the middle of his final year of high school, I was labeled a late bloomer and I wasn't accepting the fact that D1 schools weren't recruiting me. I didn't know my potential and I didn't want to limit myself by going to a school that wouldn't be fun. My foolish young mind desired the feel of the fictional "Hillman University" from the TV show, *A Different World*. I was lazy and unrealistic because I wanted the Black College experience, I wanted to be a basketball player, and I wanted to go to school for free. But the reality for that seventeen-year-old kid was that he didn't make an attempt to learn how to play the game of basketball until his senior year. I had multiple opportunities to work with coaches, to train my body; I even went to camps and underachieved because I was afraid to fail. I had no idea how to get better and it was easy for me to apply a "fixed mindset" and suggest that I was not given the physical gifts that some of my peers were blessed with.

I want to teach others how to be reminded of their own greatness without searching for the answers in other humans, or even in books. Today, kids can look up training videos and they have access to information I could have only dreamed of. The idea of a young athlete being preoccupied with video games as a pastime is very normal and popular. NBA players spend their leisure time playing games that sometimes feature themselves.

But when you aspire to be in an elite group of professional athletes, or you have a goal to become an attorney, or maybe you want to be the best physician, there has to be time spent on what you say that you want to do. And if you don't earn exactly what you set out to accomplish, there can be only one person responsible.

This is coming from someone who dedicated an immense amount of work and time into his craft of creating music. I always believed that I missed out on my basketball dream so I applied the same work ethic that I didn't use on the court to creating music. I stayed up late most nights memorizing verses, composing songs, and creating flows so that I could improve. And for years it seemed like no matter what I did, there was a lid on the ceiling of my career. I just could not break through to become popular enough to live off of making music.

So I know what it's like to feel like you do not have total control over your success. But I did have control. I controlled my narrative, my image, my mission, and the songs I chose to write and perform, but not much of that lined up with my true self and place on this planet.

Division One is a lofty aspiration, but it is an attainable one.

. . . . .

Week 17 To-Do List: Did you have a dream that seemed out of reach when you were young? If you didn't achieve it or your focus changed, write down why that dream didn't happen. List five or six reasons why the mission you had as a high school student didn't pan out. Did it make you stronger?

WEEK 18

THE PLAN

Share this with your coworker,
Show this to your man,
Send it to your homegirl,
Or someone in your fam,
I know you got a job, but if where you want to be is not exactly where you are,
What's the goal? What's the plan?
Novel? Script? Album? Degree?
Real estate license? Need to start an LLC?
Or get your MBA, are you a youngster with a dream to make it to the NBA,
NFL, MLB?
Last year you just talked, last month you slacked,
Last week you said that time is what you lacked,
Every single day you give energy to the things that you don't want in life,
maybe that's what's holding you back,
For instance, we make jokes where we call ourselves broke,
We see something disturbing, we share it and repost,
We generalize genders like all men cheat or you can't trust women so nobody
gets close,
Today you can stop finding ways to say no,
Do the podcast, or YouTube channel, create the show,
Write the book, map the steps out, you can take it slow,
But you have to plant the seed to see it grow,
And surround yourself with people with vision, That want to see you glow,
'cause if they can't see the shine in themselves, they'll block your flow,
Play this for your sister,
Send this to your bro,
Share this with your spouse or some random person you know
Or just answer this question,
How hard would you go
If you're the employee, supervisor, and CEO?
Stop playing

In 2005, I was fortunate enough to get booked to perform in Morocco. My manager Boobie Don and I were on stage in Africa receiving so much love. I believed my plan to be a superstar was working.

THE PLAN

Share this with your coworker,
Show this to your man,
Send it to your homegirl,
Or someone in your fam,
I know you got a job, but if where you want to be is not exactly where you are,
What's the goal? What's the plan?

Somebody needs to hear this. Failure to plan is a dilemma that many people are faced with. When you don't know how to create a series of action items to reach a single goal it's not always a result of procrastination or laziness, it may be because of ignorance.

I grew up in New York City where the price of living is so high that making money is the primary mission of most adults in order to survive. New York living isn't about having space or warm weather, it's about earning enough to live comfortably. I knew that if I had to live on my own in my hometown that I would sacrifice a piece of my long-term goal so I could make ends meet. I feared that once I was able to sustain myself that I would get so wrapped up in the money I would be earning, and that would cancel my dream. It's easier to blame an entire city than it is to admit that I didn't do what I needed to do by any means necessary.

Around the world, we work, we pay bills, we buy groceries to eat, we eat out at restaurants, we buy clothes, we take trips, and we say we're enjoying life but for plenty of us, weekends and vacation times are the climax of our merriment. How do you get out of the rut of a position you don't love? Ask yourself what it is that you love. Find out what makes you excited.

Novel? Script? Album? Degree?
Real estate license? Need to start an LLC?
Or get your MBA, are you a youngster with a dream to make it to the NBA, NFL, MLB?

It doesn't matter how outlandish your dream is. It is no longer a dream when you plan steps. If it's a script or a master's degree, all it takes is putting one metaphoric foot forward at a time. You may have no clue how to start a business, but it's doable when you begin the process. When you begin to research other projects like yours and then you write down your reason for embarking on the mission, your paths start to become clear.

I have a goal to create an online course for people to access. Right now, I would love to instruct others that want to learn how to write using rhyming words for rapping, singing, or poetry. Currently, I am looking at other courses that exist, I'm outlining possible chapters I would want to include, and I'm researching promotional strategies and pricing for online courses. The first part of this process is a bit vapid because I am overwhelmed with the thought of uncertainty when it comes to creating content and putting in time. But instead of focusing on the completed project, I am spotlighting the first operation in order to move on to the next one.

Last year you just talked, last month you slacked,
Last week you said that time is what you lacked,
Every single day you give energy to the things that you don't want in life, maybe that's what's holding you back,
For instance, we make jokes where we call ourselves broke,
We see something disturbing, we share it and repost,
We generalize genders like all men cheat or you can't trust women so nobody gets close,

It is so easy to talk yourself out of doing something productive. It is just as simple to be playfully negative. Someone pays you a compliment and you deflect it by diminishing your worth playfully. You mention your depleted funds as if you like being the underdog. You claim things are "tight" or you have to watch your spending for lunch, or you just simply believe that where you are financially is who you are. None of that is true.

You don't have to tell people you're struggling so they'll pity you. You don't have to share and repost that fight video or that terrible song or that thirst trapping body. And you definitely don't have to keep the opposite sex away from you because you got hurt once. Get over it all. Practice receiving compliments, work on responding to positive praises with thankfulness, and find a phrase that you can repeat in your head whenever someone pushes you to feel negative. Take the high road and make choices that reflect your intelligence. You may have to whisper to yourself, "Go high!"

Today you can stop finding ways to say no,
Do the podcast, or YouTube channel, create the show,
Write the book, map the steps out, you can take it slow,
But you have to plant the seed to see it grow,

Back in 2014, I received a message from my boy Remo stating that someone named Reggie who worked at the BET network was looking for me. Reggie was somewhat of a fan of mine and he wanted me to perform a verse on the now defunct show, *106th & Park*. I had not written any rhymes that year and I had not performed since October of 2012. I was afraid I would not be able to write something clever enough to simultaneously cater to adult fans and the youthful demographic of the show's audience.

I was making close to $24,000 per year working in the school system and coaching and I could not afford a flight to New York on such short notice. I also couldn't put myself in the rapper mode since I was not living a "rapper" life. There were so many reasons for me to turn down that offer. I was considering all of those rejection reasons as I sat in my apartment. Something inside of me shifted during my moment of silence in my home and I started to imagine positive outcomes.

What if I found the mental space to write a verse that was really good? What if I got a buddy pass and flew for cheap and I stayed with my brother Ian at his place for free while I was in New York? What if I did well and didn't stumble when delivering my verse? What if I stopped concerning myself with the outcome and just asked myself if I desired rapping for a national audience? The negative thoughts were leaving and I kept flowing with positivity until I decided to say yes and it all worked out. To this day, it was one of my best performances and I didn't care about the number of views on the video or if I sounded like an old school rapper (in my head), I was grateful to be thought of and I was thankful to be able to share my voice and messages.

The verse that I spat that day, seemed impossible to write, and once I constructed it, I didn't know how I would memorize it all. Not only did I compose something timeless, I learned each word so that my delivery looked effortless as I recited over four minutes of rhymes in one take. When you begin to break down goals and outline the necessary moves, what starts out grand and overwhelming becomes task after task until you realize you've made a huge dent in something that seemed beyond you.

And surround yourself with people with vision,
That want to see you glow, 'cause if they can't see the shine in themselves, they'll block your flow,
Play this for your sister,
Send this to your bro,
Share this with your spouse or some random person you know
Or just answer this question....
How hard would you go
If you're the employee, supervisor, and CEO?

It is important to tighten your circle as you grow. I've seen people who were best friends in college but a year or two after graduation; they are in such different places that they can't coexist. But more important than cutting people off is adding positive, like-minded, encouraging people in your life. You should be on the lookout for those that have similar values as you.

And then ask yourself the question: if you were your own boss, what would your life/work balance look like, and how successful would your company be? Would you be an independent artist, the owner of a clothing line, the head of a real estate business? Any of these positions put you at the forefront and in the driver's seat. There's no one to check your time clock to see if you showed up and put in the work. If you don't kill it, you don't eat it.

How many of us need supervisors in life? Do we need alarm clocks to wake us up and do we need monetary limits to dictate our job descriptions? What if your job was to do what you love, but in order for it to feed you and your family, *you* had to make it happen? What's the goal? Then, what's the plan?

· · · · ·

Week 18 To-Do List: If you had the opportunity to create the list of top-level employees at your workplace, who would be on your dream team? Would you choose co-workers that you have now? Would you have the same supervisor? Would you be the boss?

WEEK 19

THE PAIN

Grief, sadness, sorrow, pain
When someone close passes, it feels like permanent rain,
People send condolences,
I'm not even sure what a condolence is, but it sounds good to keep us sane,
Most of the time, friends don't know what to say,
"Keep your head up, maintain, yo, I been through the same,
Hey, I'm here if you need me,"
But do we ever say, "I'm really hurting, yes I need you??" that's lame,
It's truly not, there's nothing wrong with reaching out for some assistance,
When joy feels far in the distance,
When every time you try to snap out of it, a dark fleeting thought, brings the
cloudiness, the hurt is so persistent, it keeps coming back,
I know it's hard for us to hear,
But grown men don't communicate our fears,
Especially if the fear is dying,
It's difficult to confide in a spouse, parent, or peer and shed a tear,
So what do we do?
We hold it in, and keep it locked up like a house pet,
Covered like that plastic on your grandmother's couch set,
Fear is the opposite of love, so instead of always searching for the <u>plug</u>,
We need to look for an <u>outlet</u>,
Even if the <u>charge</u> is a whole lot of change,
That emotional strain becomes an appropriate gain,
So find someone to tell so they can be the umbrella or a shelter or the sun,
To pause the rain.

P.S to anyone that says that you can't mourn a celebrity,
Sometimes a person's fame is a small piece of their legacy,

Stars become stars because of lives they influence, when they entertain, we
feel their energy,

So I can shed a tear over Prince, Michael, Bernie Mac, Whitney,

Kobe, Gianna Bryant, Phife, Prodigy, Nipsey,

Chris Wallace, Chris Rios, Guru, Sean Price,

I can go all day with some legends that lost life,

So if you're a fan and someone dies that you truly admire,

Or you're fam of someone that expires,

Let their life inspire you,

To love more, mend broken friendships, squash beef, just elevate higher,

Do better

My Black Panther hoodie and socks are my tribute to Chadwick Boseman. Rest in Power King.

THE PAIN

Grief, sadness, sorrow, pain
When someone close passes, it feels like permanent rain,
People send condolences,
I'm not even sure what a condolence is, but it sounds good to keep us sane,

For anyone who's dealt with the loss of someone close, for a short amount of time, the pain feels uncontrollably shattering. There's a stinging jolt of pain that hits your heart when you realize you won't interact with the person anymore. And for someone attempting to console anyone dealing with loss, ironically, there's a loss for words.

Most of the time, friends don't know what to say,
"Keep your head up, maintain, yo I been through the same,
Hey I'm here if you need me,"
But do we ever say, "I'm really hurting, yes I need you??" that's lame,

Everyone handles pain differently. And there are levels of loss. Losing a parent is not the same as losing a friend. And the loss of offspring is probably the single most painful experience anyone could endure. When someone decides to share a hurting moment through social media, it's simple to click on an emoji and express concern. When someone has good news or a birthday, it's easier to do a mass acceptance of the well wishes. But when it comes to personal interactions, it gets more difficult to navigate counseling and what to say. I remember feeling like it was better to be strong than to let people in and appear as if I could not handle the pain. But strength is not always about dealing with pain alone.

It's truly not, there's nothing wrong with reaching out for some assistance,
When joy feels far in the distance,
When every time you try to snap out of it, a dark fleeting thought, brings the cloudiness, the hurt is so persistent, it keeps coming back,

Two of the reasons we hurt when someone leaves the earth too early are that we realize our own mortality and we will miss them. But it's not just missing the person; it's realizing the finality of death. It hits us that whatever future experiences we have in life will never be shared with this person. And you can't help but think about that over and over. What would they be doing now? How would they respond to something happening in our life? Did they know how much I loved them?

I know it's hard for us to hear,
But grown men don't communicate our fears,
Especially if the fear is dying,
It's difficult to confide in a spouse, parent, or peer and shed a tear,
So what do we do?
We hold it in, and keep it locked up like a house pet,
Covered like that plastic on your grandmother's couch set,
Fear is the opposite of love, so instead of always searching for the <u>plug</u>,
We need to look for an <u>outlet</u>,

This message is not just for grown men, but also for all humans who don't know how to reach out for assistance. Mental health is not something taught or mentioned in the majority of households. Schools teach math and language arts but students aren't taught how to deal with triggers or sorrow and it's spawned a generation of adults who would rather spill their deepest feelings on a Facebook wall for "friend" support before actually reaching out to a friend and having a personal conversation.

A lot of y'all are too young to know what it's like to have plastic on your furniture growing up. It was such a normal solution that it never seemed odd to us as children. A soft, plush couch or comfy chair was covered in loud, sticky, transparent plastic for years to protect the furniture from harm. There was also fear that the couch or chair would be damaged before it was fully paid for. It makes sense that a group of people that had recently acquired some equal rights would think that anything could be taken from them at any time. Whatever we deemed as sacred needed to be kept as new as possible. We were taught to treat our emotions the same way.

Even if the <u>charge</u> is a whole lot of change,
That emotional strain becomes an appropriate gain,
So find someone to tell so they can be the umbrella or a shelter or the sun,
To pause the rain,

What we fear the most when it comes to sharing is that feeling of vulnerability. Men are often misguided into believing that masculinity means you have to mask your emotions. It is hard to see how revealing a truth about yourself or tearing down a wall can lead to a spiritual breakthrough. It just doesn't sound like fun to possibly be psychoanalyzed or judged. Be aware that if at some point in your childhood, you feared sharing truths because you were ridiculed or scorned by adults, that may affect how you share your feelings today.

P.S. to anyone that says that you can't mourn a celebrity,
Sometimes a person's fame is a small piece of their legacy,
Stars become stars, because of lives they influence, when they entertain, we feel their energy,
So I can shed a tear over Prince, Michael, Bernie Mac, Whitney,
Kobe, Gianna Bryant, Phife, Prodigy, Nipsey,
Chris Wallace, Chris Rios, Guru, Sean Price,
I can go all day with some legends that lost life,

So if you're a fan and someone dies that you truly admire,
Or you're fam of someone that expires,
Let their life inspire you,
To love more, mend broken friendships, squash beef, just elevate higher,
Do better

I wrote this after the passing of Kobe and Gianna Bryant. I am a huge fan of Kobe Bryant, the man and the ballplayer. To this day, I am still processing the loss of someone I never met but felt deeply connected to. I felt the same feeling when Chadwick Boseman passed away. I don't necessarily view celebrities as people that we are not allowed to mourn if we don't know them personally. The reason we consider them celebrities is because whatever talent or skill they possess has reached the masses. To me, it means that the energy they released to the world is powerful. And we all have a right to miss their contribution and feel for the families that knew them personally. Someone might need to hear that.

· · · · ·

Week 19 To-Do List: Have you ever given deep consideration to what happens when we pass away? Whether you have or you haven't, write down what you think occurs when our bodies no longer serve an earthly purpose. And then write your own eulogy if that's not too creepy. Maybe you can jot a few sentences that speak to the type of person you are and how people will remember you. Are you living a life that is consistent with what you want that memory to be?

WEEK 20

THE VICTIM EYES

I told y'all before the internal battle is gory,

Inside of our heads, we make up our own stories,

But everything happening to me,

It wasn't happening to me, it was actually, truly happening for me,

So who needs to hear that?

Since last time it missed them,

It's tough to get those habits out of your system,

Someone is always doing you wrong,

You keep getting hated on,

Relationships start out strong,

But then you turn into the victim,

And every single time that there's fault, or there's blame,

You attach it to a human that does not have your name,

The one you thought was the one, keeps playing games,

Your supervisor, fuels your fire, driving you insane,

The clouds don't just follow you when it rains,

But it's harder to make a change than it is to complain,

I hate to break the news, but the one causing the issues, and the person reporting them are the same,

We all know folks out there that continue to live the lies,

They walk inside a room and can instantly switch the vibe,

They're broke and they're tired, but somehow energized,

To tell job sob stories with hopes that you empathize,

They can't even visualize

A happy ending

Because the glass is constantly half-empty in a victim's eyes,

How can you attack your goals when you're always victimized?

Your problems look colossal,

Your accomplishments get minimized,
Every day you lift your eyes,
Please be accountable,
If you badmouth and vilify,
The people around you,
And then use "I statements,"
"I've been bitter," "I was jaded,"
I chose this path, this is what I created,
Any missteps on the way, yes I've made them,
But I'm still God's child, in His eyes, I'm high favored,
I am not a victim!

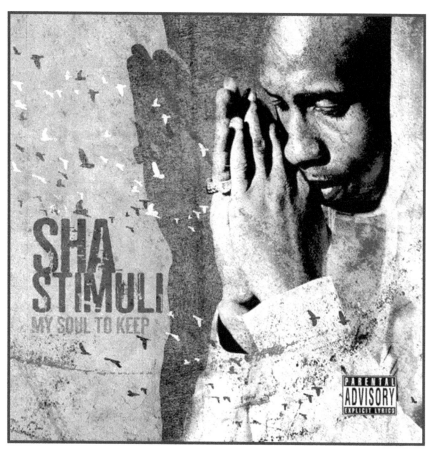

In 2009 I released my debut album *My Soul To Keep* on E1 Records. I was in a dark place while I was writing and recording this album. When I listen to it I can feel my sadness. The title suggested that I was holding onto my soul in an evil industry. I was the victim.

THE VICTIM EYES

I told y'all before the internal battle is gory,
Inside of our heads, we make up our own stories,
But everything happening to me,
It wasn't happening to me, it was actually, truly happening for me,

I touched on this before but this writing is going a little deeper. As we evolve and endure trials that make us stronger and shape our character, we sometimes feel as though life is the assailant and we are walking around waiting for the world to throw turmoil at us. Even if you've survived through some unforeseen hardships, there is still some light ahead.

So who needs to hear that?
Since last time it missed them,
It's tough to get those habits out of your system,
Someone is always doing you wrong,
You keep getting hated on,
Relationships start out strong,
But then you turn into the victim,
And every single time that there's fault or there's blame,
You attach it to a human that does not have your name,
The one you thought was the one keeps playing games,
Your supervisor fuels your fire, driving you insane,
The clouds don't just follow you when it rains,
But it's harder to make a change than it is to complain,
I hate to break the news, but the one causing the issues and the person reporting them are the same,

There was a time in my life when I felt like the universe was working against me. I was transitioning into a full-time independent artist but I didn't have a solid fan base, and mostly, I didn't have consistent income. During this time, my music reflected the attitude that I had adopted. Most of my verses and songs circled around the topic of the music industry not letting me in, people not liking me, the South's emergence in the genre, or the fact that hip-hop was no longer the pure, authentic brand that it had appeared to be when I was younger.

But the truth is hip-hop always had balance and the more it grew, the more artists were pressured to generate dollars with their product. It was a natural progression and my lack of attention to the marketing side of my image left me feeling like the talented victim who would often refer to himself as an underdog. I was even working on a project, *Cinderella Man*, named after the Russell Crowe movie about the boxer no one believed in until poverty forced him to improve himself and win.

I was yearning for tragedy and triumph. I did not have the mental capacity to embrace what I was experiencing. I tried many times but I just kept going back to blaming the world, the rap game, the fans, and people that were supposed to guide my career instead of having a gritty talk with the mirror. I even pointed the finger at my girl and I created the narrative in my head that she wanted me to quit music. I was walking around with victim eyes.

We all know folks out there that continue to live the lies,
They walk inside a room and can instantly switch the vibe,
They're broke and they're tired, but somehow energized,
To tell job sob stories with hopes that you empathize,
They can't even visualize
A happy ending,
Because the glass is constantly half-empty in a victim's eyes,

I can say for a fact that I could not see a happy ending in my music career, and in some ways, my life. I wanted success but I couldn't put my sights on it. All I could see was that there would be a time when I would no longer walk the earth and that would cause people to search my name on the Internet, memorialize me, and then finally like my music.

We have all been around people that can never say their day is going great. The weather could be phenomenal or they may have just received a paycheck and you would expect them to be glowing with positivity. Instead, they easily shun the beauty of the day and find a reason to be unhappy.

How can you attack your goals when you're always victimized?
Your problems look colossal,
Your accomplishments get minimized,

It is so easy to worry and be afraid. There was a time when I would wake up and try to remember everything I had on my plate that was causing me strife. I would wake up feeling sleepy because my alarm went off. And right away I started thinking:

"Man, there used to be a time when I could sleep all day."

"I should go back to sleep and take the day off."

"I can't believe I have a job and I'm not making a lot of money. I don't even feel like getting dressed."

"How am I going to afford the rent this month?"

I would just keep going and spiral into the abyss of negativity before something like food would take my mind off my issues. I couldn't even be joyful about having a son because I was so worried about how I would provide. Would my wife think I'm a failure because of my paycheck? Can we afford our apartment and two cars and daycare?

I shed tears the first day I had to drop my son Zaire off at daycare back in 2016. Not because I was worried about him, but because he was only four months old, my wife was going back to work after maternity leave, and I felt guilty that I couldn't stay home and be with him. I berated myself and felt that if I had been a successful rap artist I would be able to own my day, I would have enough money to support my family, and my son would be able to stay home for the first year of his life.

I was an imaginary victim of circumstance and I was focusing on anything negative. I was unsure about the path I had embarked on, and in the back of my mind, it wasn't my fault for my situation. I didn't have a "why" or a purpose because the move to get into education wasn't planned. At the time, I was there because I needed stability and the school system was a way to maintain myself and have minimal, seasonal freedom.

But as time passed and I affected more lives, I began to embrace the students I met and the teachable moments we shared. They weren't just people I was passing by on my way to the next stage of life. They were instrumental in my life. I remember donating a microphone to some students that rapped but didn't have a place to record. I can recall a time where I was the sounding board for a young girl who was being bullied by her classmates. I consoled, I comforted, I trained, I tutored, I assisted, I gave myself without a concern that anything would be reciprocated other than the rewarding feeling I felt that was more fulfilling than a fan messaging me that my verse was hot. My days were filled with accomplishments, both theirs and mine, that were giving me clarity. I had to recognize and allow these students to guide me to a place of gratitude and joy.

Everyday you lift your eyes,
Please be accountable,
If you badmouth and vilify,
The people around you,
And then use "I statements,"
"I've been bitter, I was jaded,
I chose this path, this is what I created,
Any missteps on the way, yes I've made them,
But I'm still God's child, in His eyes, I'm high favored,
I am not a victim!

"I statements." One of the most difficult processes involved on the road to self-enlightenment is to reframe every statement that expresses feelings or thoughts with the pronoun "I" in front of the sentence. It's the same practice used in marital counseling and therapy. Owning feelings is not easy when you're accustomed to projecting and blaming others. You are highly favored and loved. No matter how trying the times feel, your energy can switch at any time and you will know that the universe is not out to get you.

· · · · ·

Week 20 To-Do List: Think of something that happened in your life that didn't have the best possible outcome. And then think about how you attracted it. I'm not talking about the death of a loved one or a serious illness. I'm talking about a job loss or a failed audition, a break-up, an argument, or a financial hole. Get that unpleasant incident in your head and try to tell the story to an imaginary stranger, but only use "I statements."

Even if someone else played a role in your story, start with "I" and own your reaction to it. It sounds simple, but it can be a real challenge if you're used to pointing the finger at others for your mishaps or wrongdoings.

WEEK 21

THE MIRROR

One thing that's embarrassing that I used to be guilty of
Was when I saw one of my peers or colleagues getting love,
I would smile in their face and appear to big them up,
But in my head, behind their back, I'd be thinking different stuff like,
"He doesn't go as hard as me,"
"He's not that good,"
"If I had what he had, I would stand where he stood,"
Instead of, "Can, Will, Do," I was, "Should, Would, Could,"
You know that crab mentality that keeps us in the hood,
Your boy is getting recruited and y'all got the same stats,
Your homie's music is trending but you write the better raps,
Your bestie found a man, there is so much that she lacks,
While you're perfect and still single,
But you can't find your match,
You know people like that, the victory could be clear-cut,
They still have to come up with a, "Yeah, but"
"Yeah, but he ain't really getting it,"
"Yeah, but will it last?"
"Yeah, he's hot now, but I knew him when he was trash,"
"Yeah, but she was raised with two parents,
They gave her cash and made sure she went to class and passed,"
Don't let the past dictate your reaction or emotion,
Congratulate your peeps on their business or their promotion,
Their award, their love, their baby, their success,
Just because they get more, it doesn't leave you with less,
If somebody else eats, that doesn't make you starve,
When someone makes a deposit, it won't make you withdraw,
If your boy landed a role or your friend got a new car,
Wherever that person's at, it doesn't change where you are,
That's on you!

My wedding day was November 14th, 2014. I was facing the mirror and I was finally admiring the person I saw.

THE MIRROR

One thing that's embarrassing that I used to be guilty of
Was when I saw one of my peers or colleagues getting love,
I would smile in their face, and appear to big them up,
But in my head, behind their back, I'd be thinking different stuff like,
"He doesn't go as hard as me,"
"He's not that good,"
"If I had what he had, I would stand where he stood,"
Instead of, "Can, Will, Do," I was, "Should, Would, Could,"
You know that crab mentality that keeps us in the hood,

This is honestly embarrassing because I can remember what it felt like when I would look on HipHopGame.com (thanks to this book's editor Brian Kayser) and some of the rappers that I thought I was better than were getting way more "listens" on their songs. Some of them had a heaping amount of MySpace friends and at the time, that was a big deal. Can you see how crazy that is? Years ago, I was worried about my MySpace friend count. Today, people are observing followers and views religiously, but one day none of that will matter.

It's counterproductive to make up excuses in your head why someone else is excelling. Even if I didn't say it out loud, I acknowledged that I was a quiet hater. I couldn't understand why people with less content and more gimmicks were winning. I couldn't grasp the fact that there were artists that followed my blueprint for releasing content online before it was a mainstream practice and that they were drastically more successful than me.

One day, I received a message from a college student who told me he was contemplating suicide. He said that one of my songs, "Good Day," actually made him feel like life wasn't that bad. He went into details about the story I constructed and how it reminded him to be thankful for each day and his small victories. "Good Day" is about a young couple in a car accident that was fatal for the wife but she was expecting, and her baby survived. The student wanted to know if it was a true story. I was afraid to tell him that it was inspired by reality but most of the narrative was fictional. I kept the dialogue going with him through Facebook for a few weeks and that's when it hit me that none of the numbers of listens or followers mattered. Numbers represent people and each person is important. Whether I received 100,000 views on a video or only two, the point is that someone watched. I created intellectual property and I was able to release it to the masses while sitting in my home. How could I be concerned with the moves of another human when I was literally affecting lives with my words?

Your boy is getting recruited and y'all got the same stats,
Your homie's music is trending but you write the better raps,
Your bestie found a man, there is so much that she lacks,
While you're perfect and still single,
But you can't find your match,

These are all common scenarios where we take the opportunity to go low and give out negative energy. It's the ego's way of finding peace with what it may deem as failure or jealousy.

I met a young rapper from St. Louis named Prince Ea back in 2009 and I was blown away by his intelligence and skill. We became cool with each other and recorded some songs together, and when he visited Atlanta, we shot a video for our song entitled "Effortless."

I don't know if he considered me a mentor but I like to think I assisted with some of his early moves in the industry. I knew he was destined for greatness and my intuition proved to be correct because right now he is a world famous content creator with millions of followers, subscribers, and views on his enlightening videos that inspired me to step outside of the rapper realm. Prince Ea and I were conversing one day and I complimented him on his latest visual. I can't remember which one it was but he always has well-produced and thought out concepts that touch the viewers' hearts and minds. His response to my laudation was interesting. He said that the video wasn't doing as well as some others; it only had a few hundred thousand views. I tried to keep my composure as I chuckled a little at his attempt at modesty. In my head I thought about what it would feel like to have one million views as the benchmark for any visual I released. I felt silly and small because I was supposed to be the big brother, the accomplished former signed artist but Ea had taken the baton and achieved major success.

I was happy for him but his statement taught me two things. One of those lessons was that I should never compare another person's journey to my own. We all move at different speeds, we're inspired by various muses, and we can never be aware of someone else's struggles. Then there was the fact that no matter how popular or successful I might be, there is always another level to be desired. There's a standard set when the first book does well, when the last song released goes viral, or when you expect results similar to what you've previously accomplished. Prince Ea wasn't attempting to gloat nor was he dishonest about his feelings about the video, but I can empathize with what it feels like to try to keep up with your own efforts.

You know people like that, the victory could be clear-cut,
They still have to come up with a, "Yeah but"
"Yeah, but he ain't really getting it,"
"Yeah, but will it last?"
"Yeah, he's hot now, but I knew him when he was trash,"
"Yeah, but she was raised with two parents,
They gave her cash and made sure she went to class and passed,"

Don't be a "Yeah, but" person. When you hear about someone's good fortune or talent, you don't have to add a qualifier to it. For four years, I coached high school basketball and during and after that time, I trained students. Ever since BallIsLife.com started to put together mixtapes of high school athlete highlights, kids became obsessed with watching the best moments from ranked players.

When I was in high school, we heard about great players but we didn't have videos of every All-American basketball player across the nation. I didn't want to be a fan of someone in the same grade as me but this is a new generation of ballers that have no issue with idolizing their peers. As I trained them, I would reference the work ethic of a popular, highly recruited student in an attempt to motivate a trainee. One of my students would reply with a, "Yeah, but" and then they'd proceed to tell me that the ranked player is taller, stronger, and probably has a full-time trainer.

They would always have a reason that a student who is better than them had an unfair advantage. It is rare for a kid to say that another young man is better because they worked harder than them. And to be honest, I was the same way. Even in adulthood, I've done the same thing.

Don't let the past dictate your reaction or emotion,

It is now time to rewrite my story. I can't go back and change how I used to react to other people's successes. I can only move forward from a place of extreme gratitude for my own accomplishments and perhaps even more importantly, I can celebrate other's victories.

Congratulate your peeps on their business or their promotion,
Their award, their love, their baby, their success,
Just because they get more, it doesn't leave you with less,
If somebody else eats, that doesn't make you starve,
When someone makes a deposit, it won't make you withdraw,
If your boy landed a role, or your friend got a new car,
Wherever that person's at, it doesn't change where you are,
That's on you!

I mentioned that I minored in Theatrical Arts at Delaware State University but what I did not point out was that I never took my minor seriously. I wanted to be famous enough doing music that I could simply get any acting role because of my status. That didn't work out so I used to secretly envy my peers who chased their dreams and landed acting roles. I would say to myself that I was better than them even though I wasn't.

When I first moved to Atlanta, I called my mother and asked her to help me pay for an acting class. She obliged, and for three months I was at The Company Acting Studio learning techniques and performing in the beginner class. Two months in, I became the star of the class. I was the only one who could memorize material in less than an hour. I took direction really well and my monologues were powerful. At the end of the three months, the instructor pulled me to the side after class and told me she thought I should audition for the master class. I smiled. I was thrilled beyond belief. And I never took another acting class. I had fulfilled my mission to learn the craft and I knew that I could be good at it with more training. But at that time, coaching high school basketball, getting back with Azizi, and making quality use of my free time was more important than becoming an actor. I knew that if I pursued an acting career, I would have gone extremely hard. It wasn't time for that to happen. But the instructor's recommendation gave me the peace I needed to congratulate my boys sincerely when they get booked for something. I want to see them win and when my time comes to be in front of the camera, I shall be ready. It's your turn.

· · · · ·

Week 21 To-Do List: Write down the names of five people in your circle that you are proud of and why. "I am proud of my best friend because_____." Were you always in a space where you had no problem with congratulating your friends for their accomplishments? Explain why or why not.

WEEK 22

THE MAGIC

Somebody told me that *The Secret* wasn't working,

They couldn't apply the tactic,

Of visualizing any desire so they attract it,

I told them that the author of *The Secret* said the habits that you need to pull it off, involve *The Magic*,

They asked, "What's that?"

I said, "*The Magic* is something all of us practice,

But all you need to do is just turn it up and be active,"

A lot of us are captives, trapped inside these moments where we can't see the goodness we already have captured,

I know I'm taking long, but the process to master

The Magic might just seem backwards,

For example, if you want more money, the way to extract it,

Is be thankful for the amount of money that you can access,

You have a high rent or mortgage; just switch your reaction,

If you have the means to pay it, you should feel satisfaction,

You have a car note that's hefty,

Thank the bank, thank insurance, thank the car company because they manufactured it,

It's just like blessing your food before you digest it,

That small amount of time that you're investing,

That's the same magical energy consistently affecting,

The way your food keeps on coming, apply that method,

To your bills, to your grocery shopping, traveling expenses,

Wardrobe, shoe game, then you just extend it

To your home, health, and wellness,

Then get intense with it,

Once you have the power of gratitude, it's endless,

Be grateful for your friends that are positivity magnets,

Be thankful for the breath in your lungs each day that you have it,

If you want to settle debt,

Or you're yearning a life that's lavish,

Be more grateful for what you already attracted and that's *The Magic*.

My current home in Atlanta, Georgia. Years ago, I couldn't imagine living in a space like this. I can't fathom what my next residence might look like. I am grateful.

THE MAGIC

Somebody told me that The Secret *wasn't working,*
They couldn't apply the tactic,
Of visualizing any desire so they attract it,

It is quite possible that some of the most important pieces of information I've received in my adult life came from non-fiction, self-help books. *A New Earth, Conversations With God, Blink, The Road Less Traveled,* and *The Secret* all helped me go within to solve the enlightenment equation. Implementing *The Secret* can boost highly pleasurable outcomes, but limitless potential and consistent alignment with Source energy takes some deep soul-searching that I didn't find in that literature.

I told them that the author of The Secret *said the habits that you need to pull it off,*
involve The Magic,
They asked, "What's that?"
*I said, "*The Magic *is something all of us practice,*
But all you need to do is just turn it up and be active,"
A lot of us are captives, trapped inside these moments where we can't see the goodness
we already have captured,

I was in a FedEx store returning my equipment to AT&T because I had finally gotten rid of cable. My wife and I kept hitting a wall every month where our income wasn't covering bills. We were pulling from savings, our joint account would get overdraft fees, we had our baby's surgery, a major plumbing issue, and her vehicle needed a big repair to get on the road. Through it all, we had fleeting thoughts of, *Can we handle this house?* We figured that we needed to cut expenses so we looked at finances and started trimming.

We kept perspective and stayed optimistic and didn't point any fingers or blame at ourselves. And then I saw it...*The Magic.* It was in a similar font as *The Secret* so I picked it up due to my curiosity. I stumbled upon a passage that talked about being grateful for health when you're healthy. The author mentioned the magic being the act of gratitude and I thought to myself, *I'm already extremely grateful.* When I exercise I don't count reps, I just repeat that I'm grateful and I think about everything that got me where I am. I assumed that my method of meditation mixed with callisthenic workouts was enough to show my gratitude.

The Magic book contains more insight and delves deeper into what it means to express gratitude. Author Rhonda Byrne laid out a plan to ensure that gratitude becomes an action. I wanted to feel the feeling she wrote about. I wanted to turn up the magic and see where it landed me. I didn't buy the book. But when I got home, I kept thinking about it. So I tried to find the audio version. There wasn't one. I checked Amazon Prime and there it was. I ordered it.

I know I'm taking long, but the process to master
The Magic *might just seem backwards,*
For example, if you want more money, the way to extract it,
Is be thankful for the amount of money that you can access,
You have a high rent or mortgage, just switch your reaction,
If you have the means to pay it, you should feel satisfaction,
You have a car note that's hefty,
Thank the bank, thank insurance, thank the car company because they manufactured it,

What was so special about this woman's words that I couldn't figure out on my own? The thing is I had already figured it out. I just needed to apply it to everything. I hadn't considered all the levels of people, and occurrences, and parts of nature that all move accordingly and daily to satisfy all of my tiny needs and desires. The space I reside in, the Internet I use, the food I consume, the office I work in, the car I drive, and all of these things don't exist without someone else's effort. Humans and nature come together and use resources to provide beautiful, tasteful experiences that we may not take for granted, but we don't necessarily acknowledge. And that's where the magic comes in. Rhonda Byrne provides a chance for readers to dedicate time and energy to being thankful. I needed that.

It's just like blessing your food before you digest it,
That small amount of time that you're investing,
That's the same magical energy consistently affecting,
The way your food keeps on coming, apply that method,
To your bills, to your grocery shopping, traveling expenses,
Wardrobe, shoe game, then you just extend it
To your home, health and wellness,
Then get intense with it,
Once you have the power of gratitude, it's endless,

Money is usually our biggest target when it comes to attraction, but how often do you consider the amount of money that has passed through your fingers in your life? How many millions do you think you've had access to since you were a child? You spent double-digit years of your life not paying for anything and yet you still ate, bathed, lived somewhere, had clothes, and schooling. That was all free of charge, and then you started making money. And you still are. Even if you're not making the kind of money you want to right now, the fact that you've had access to so much money over the span of your life is enough to shed a gratitude-filled tear.

Be grateful for your friends that are positivity magnets,
Be thankful for the breath in your lungs each day that you have it,
If you want to settle debt,
Or you're yearning a life that's lavish,
Be more grateful for what you already attracted and that's The Magic.

Another tactic that amazes me about Rhonda Byrne's book is she asks the reader to create lists. As you can see I studied and am inspired by her writings. She asks for lists of blessings and sometimes lists of humans. Humans that allowed your life to have ease and some that influenced you, even some that you have a conflict with. Reading the book caused me to think about my friends who are true positive individuals.

I thought about the ones that may not be close friends or acquaintances but whenever I speak to them, their energy is high and I feel empowered by their presence. I thought more about the bodily functions that I don't give attention to. I thought about my moving legs, wandering eyes, lungs filled with air, digestive system, and blood flowing everywhere that I need it. We need to praise all of the marvelous working parts that come together to keep us alive and functioning. Be grateful for them and watch the magic work for you.

· · · · ·

Week 22 To-Do List: I want you to think about some people and things that you are grateful for. But I want you to focus solely on the physical space you are in at the moment. Look around and write down five things that you are grateful for that you can put eyes on right now. If you have more than five, feel free to keep going. You can also create another list every day this week. Continue to express gratitude as much as possible until it's a way of life.

WEEK 23

THE MANTRA

I used to go to church,

I doubted my self-worth,

My whole life, I've been hearing, "Put God first,"

People love to say it, like a slogan when you're voting,

But nobody tells you how putting God first works,

At six, I thought it meant go to school and have good behavior,

At twelve, I figured it was accept Christ as my savior,

Here I am, over three decades later,

And I'm still not sure but I need a small favor,

When you put God first, tell me how does that translate?

Are Good Samaritan actions inside of the mandate?

Does how you move at your job become a part of the landscape?

And how you treat folks doing well or in bad shape,

To me it's like a mental contract where you add faith,

In every situation, you can't hate,

'Cause God is love

So when you get some sad feelings you can't shake,

There's peace when you go through tough times and bad breaks,

No matter who you talk to, or what's their occupation,

Comedian or custodian, if they work in education,

Or fast food, if you act rude and show off your impatience,

That's not walking in the light of the Lord,

What I'm saying is,

God-first is a <u>mindset</u>

If every day's a <u>battle</u>, all around you there's <u>mines set</u>,

Step on one and you <u>explode</u>, switch your mode, lose control, doesn't matter how hard the grind gets,

Putting God first doesn't mean you strictly live by the word,

And it doesn't mean your spouse or your kids come third,
It just means that life decisions,
Practical or absurd,
All get governed by one rule we all should learn,
Move with Love

We met in high school in 1992 and we rekindled at the high school reunion in 2005. In 2006 she met my family and we were going to church together. This is Greater Mount Pleasant in Brooklyn, New York, the first church I attended and sang in the choir at 5 years old. I don't know who that dude was that photobombed us.

THE MANTRA

I used to go to church,
I doubted my self-worth,
My whole life, I've been hearing, "Put God first,"
People love to say it, like a slogan when you're voting,
But nobody tells you how putting God first works,

I remember being a child watching awards shows with my family and whenever the award winner gave a speech; my mom would listen to make sure they thanked God first. If they didn't, she would have something to say. She didn't say anything demeaning, but she would suggest that nothing could be done without The Creator. She did the same for sports interviews when players would thank people and start with their mom, dad, and coaches.

On the flipside, whenever someone thanked God first, she would nod and even applaud them for recognizing on such a large platform that they acknowledged a higher power. "That's right!" she would bellow when they got it right. This was the definition of putting God first to me when I was a child. It made perfect sense.

At six, I thought it meant go to school and have good behavior,
At twelve, I figured it was accept Christ as my savior,
Here I am, over three decades later,
And I'm still not sure but I need a small favor,

Once I learned that putting God first wasn't such a literal statement, I started to make sure that my actions aligned with what I felt in my heart. I realized that saying grace before I ate was a small part of the process, because it was technically placing God before eating meals. I also figured out that repenting and accepting Christ as my savior could put me in a strong position. And just to be safe, I decided that if I ever became an award winner, my parents would come second in my acknowledgements. I still wanted to dig deeper and get to the true core of the mantra.

When you put God first, tell me how does that translate?
Are Good Samaritan actions inside of the mandate?
Does how you move at your job become a part of the landscape?
And how you treat folks doing well or in bad shape,

Here's where we get to the important part of the process. I asked myself the questions that can turn a group of words into a way of life. I wonder if putting God first is the key to becoming a better person, and does it include integrity and being kind to all groups of individuals. The mission is to reach a godly level of consciousness.

To me it's like a mental contract where you add faith,
In every situation, you can't hate,
'Cause God is love
So when you get some sad feelings, you can't shake,
There's peace when you go through tough times and bad breaks,
No matter who you talk to, or what's their occupation,
Comedian or custodian, if they work in education,
Or fast food, if you act rude and show off your impatience,
That's not walking in the light of the Lord,
What I'm saying is,

It took me some time but instead of figuring out what the term means to others, I defined it for myself. And that meaning is simply replacing the word "God" with the word, "love." When it comes to actions, choices, and deeds, there is no better way to decide how to move and how to treat others like infusing love.

God-first is a mindset
If every day's a battle, all around you there's mines set,
Step on one and you explode, switch your mode,
Lose control, doesn't matter how hard the grind gets,
Putting God first doesn't mean you strictly live by the word,
And it doesn't mean your spouse or your kids come third,

It just means that life decisions,
Practical or absurd,
All get governed by one rule we all should learn,
Move with Love

There will always be triggers and events that take you out of a peaceful place. In those moments, it is hard to act with the best intentions in mind that mirror The Almighty. We are not perfect beings and we should not expect to always turn the other cheek. Nor should we ignore the needs of our loved ones or take the scriptures as strict guidelines. Your choices are all you have in this world and once you peel back the layers of your intentions, you can create a powerful habit of injecting positivity and love in all that you do. That is truly putting God first.

· · · · ·

Week 23 To-Do List: Think about some scenarios that could have been affected if you changed the way you approached them. Write down three times you had an unfavorable outcome and what you could have done to emit a higher vibration. Elaborate on what happened and how love can change your actions.

WEEK 24

THE DAILY SERMON

Sunday morning when you sit inside the pews,
And you hear the pastor, preacher, reverend,
Talk the talk and spark the fuse,
Light the match and give you that peaceful energy you can use,
When you go out in the world, those teachings become your muse,
The services aren't about your dress, hair, or your shoes,
If your cleavage is exposed or if you're showing your tattoos,
If you give a healthy blessing when they pass around collection,
Or whatever you give is for you to choose,
It doesn't change your afterlife status,
There are no points you can lose,
God doesn't keep score,
I used to get confused,
I was afraid if I hadn't been to church in awhile,
But then I'd see churchgoers in the streets moving wild,
I didn't judge 'em, I just wondered was Sunday worship a style,
Or a fad, either way, it made me go the extra mile,
Because I felt like a fraud, just surviving, existing,
My daily actions didn't derive from a mission,
Not dying is different from really living,
Man, I wasn't living, until I got fired from just rhyming about violence and
women,
My climate would shift and my mindset would lift,
I got hired to give people knowledge and vision,
I took a higher position,
It's your turn,
Don't treat God like a conjugal visit,
Who comes Sunday morning when your heart is exquisite,

Your talk is efficient; your walk is persistent,

By Wednesday or Thursday, She's gone, and you're toxic, dismissive,

And making rash, low-logic decisions,

Be careful that praying does not become some recycled tradition,

This might upset you and incite some division,

But what if one day you found out that the Bible was fiction?

Sort of like Greek Mythology inside of the scriptures,

Do you really need a "good book" to guide your intentions?

Are you mad at that question?

Are you rattled with tension?

I don't mean to minimize the holy valuable lessons,

I just want you to do some deep active reflection,

Are you carrying out the deeds being spat by the reverend?

I guess an easy way to say it; do your own intervention,

Don't just post a couple of psalms for your public perception,

If you're not living what you're spitting, then cut the deception,

Right now is the perfect time to show off your imperfection,

And everyday there should be moral progression,

So don't stop paying offerings and tithes,

Just pay more attention,

To yourself

L to R. My mommy Ruby Williams, Little Sherod, Reggie "Lord Digga" Ellis (my brother) and my first cousin Brian Green. I think it was Easter Sunday in 1978 and we were in front of my Nana's house headed to church in Miami, Florida.

THE DAILY SERMON

Sunday morning when you sit inside the pews,
And you hear the pastor, preacher, reverend,
Talk the talk and spark the fuse,
Light the match and give you that peaceful energy you can use,
When you go out in the world, those teachings become your muse,

This may be my most controversial piece of writing in this collection. It is not meant to offend anyone. I wrote this in an attempt to provoke thought and, as always, speak to myself. I view the role of the leader of a church congregation as somewhat of a teacher and a catalyst setting off a week of positivity and inspiring actions.

Their sermons are meant to jar you into a mode of spiritual action and serve as a reminder for alignment with the eternal Source energy. This may be a built-up idea of what church means to me since I became an adult but it makes sense that throughout the week, if there's a point where you feel down, lost, or angered, you can refer to something derived from the scriptures to put you back on the uplifting spiritual path.

The services aren't about your dress, hair, or your shoes,
If your cleavage is exposed, or if you're showing your tattoos,
If you give a healthy blessing when they pass around collection,
Or whatever you give is for you to choose,
It doesn't change your afterlife status,
There are no points you can lose,
God doesn't keep score,
I used to get confused,
I was afraid if I hadn't been to church in awhile,
But then I'd see churchgoers in the streets moving wild,
I didn't judge 'em, I just wondered was Sunday worship a style,
Or a fad, either way, it made me go the extra mile,

I remember going to different church services in Atlanta, Georgia back in 2007. My future wife and I went to some small ones where the pressure was on to remain attentive and stay for the entire service because everyone was able to see each other in the tiny venue.

Then there was the mega church that felt like Baptists on steroids with the big screen, epic choir and band, and there was a line to get inside.

It wasn't just the size of the church that had me feeling a bit disconnected, it was me; I was used to long drawn out services with elderly ladies catching the spirit, a lot of singing, numerous prayers, all while fatigue and hunger battled for my attention. I brought that doubtful energy right into the house of worship in Atlanta and it made me notice every low-cut, tight dress, every extended hymn, the overacting congregation members, and the misinformed men at the podiums who didn't address their flock like they were adults living in the world. They spoke to them as if they were children who couldn't interpret the scriptures and needed to be afraid of hell's wrath in order to do good deeds.

Then there were the overbearing, holy rollers that criticized LeBron James for his King James nickname, or those who took subliminal jabs at homosexuals.

At one point, my main concerns were the freshness of my kicks, if my gear was dressy enough, and if I had enough cash to give as an offering. I judged people I knew that were faithful Sunday worshippers but didn't necessarily live a saintly life the other days of the week. It is safe to say I walked inside of those buildings with a cloudy mind and a mission to entertain myself rather than fulfill my soul with something enlightening.

Because I felt like a fraud, just surviving, existing,
My daily actions didn't derive from a mission,
Not dying is different from really living,
Man, I wasn't living, until I got fired from just rhyming about violence and women,
My climate would shift and my mindset would lift,

I got hired to give people knowledge and vision,
I took a higher position,

Enlightenment doesn't happen overnight. It is through time and experience that actions change, habits form, and character traits evolve. The words I chose to put on top of instrumentals were always true to me. The problem with the choices I made was my reason for using the words. My soul was crying to be a voice for the voiceless. I entered the music business hoping to bring honesty and vulnerability to rap music but I had strayed from that mission once I switched my attention to becoming popular.

It wasn't until my own songs made me cringe that I noticed I was growing as an individual. Before I became a husband and a father, I decided to release 12 EPs in 12 months in 2012. It wasn't the first time that I had done monthly projects. In 2008, DJ Victorious and I put out 12 mixtapes. It was a draining experience that I vowed never to do again. But in 2011, I felt as though I was done with rapping and I wanted to vent and release everything that I was going through. As I began to let everything out, it was refreshing to listen back as though I wasn't the creator of the music. Halfway through the year, I was no longer using profanity, the N-word was gone from my catalog, and every verse was purposeful. In 2013, I backed up so far from writing rhymes that it gave me an intense sense of clarity that I hadn't been able to find for years.

By the time I started composing again, I was a husband, I was about to be a father, and I had no intention or plan to release the music. I was just using the booth as a tool to get out my fears, frustrations, and ideas. Without trying, my approach to creating music had shifted because who I had become was a new individual. I can't identify when the switch got flipped but it makes me very appreciative that I was given so much time to find myself.

It's your turn,
Don't treat God like a conjugal visit,
Who comes Sunday morning when your heart is exquisite,
Your talk is efficient; your walk is persistent,

By Wednesday or Thursday, She's gone, and you're toxic, dismissive,
And making rash, low-logic decisions,
Be careful that praying does not become some recycled tradition,

This next group of sentences comes from a place of love and consideration. Unfortunately, when you point out truths, some view it as unfair criticism. I have friends and I am related to human beings that are avid churchgoers and scripture-spitters. I have no issue with someone who takes their faith seriously. I am also a witness to those same friends and family when they exhibit selfishness, combative characteristics, and egotistical moves without any flexibility.

Again, no one has to turn the other cheek every time there's a confrontation, but there has to be a better way for those that claim to love The Lord, for them to continue to be in a righteous mode all week and into the weekend.

I understand what it's like to get a boost of bliss and joy on Sunday and leave service feeling like I need to feed the homeless and tell everyone I love them daily. I also know how easy it is to slip into a sunken place where you're ready to engage in verbal back and forth or violence for something that does not seem logical.

This might upset you and incite some division,
But what if one day you found out that the Bible was fiction?
Sort of like Greek Mythology inside of the scriptures,
Do you really need a "good book" to guide your intentions?
Are you mad at that question?
Are you rattled with tension?
I don't mean to minimize the holy valuable lessons,
I just want you to do some deep active reflection,
Are you carrying out the deeds being spat by the reverend?
I guess an easy way to say it; do your own intervention,
Don't just post a couple of psalms for your public perception,
If you're not living what you're spitting, then cut the deception,
Right now is the perfect time to show off your imperfection,

And everyday there should be moral progression,
So don't stop paying offerings and tithes,
Just pay more attention,
To yourself

It's easy to overreact to someone asking you to view The Holy Bible as a fictional piece of literature. The Good Book is in every hotel room, church, and is the best-selling book of all time. It holds the moral guidelines and possibly historic narratives that have been passed down for generations. So why would someone ask you to look at this spiritual reference data as a novel compared to Greek mythology?

Whenever I read stories about Zeus, Ares, Aphrodite, and Hades, to name a few, I'm focused on the underlying meanings that the authors meant to convey. I don't believe that these gods were actual celestial beings that inhabited the earth but I do believe that the characteristics of these gods exist in humans. If I had to ask a devout religious follower if they believed there was really a talking serpent, a burning bush, hair that was connected to physical strength, and a man who could bring people back from the dead, the answer would probably be a resounding yes. And that affirmation would be because it came from The Bible. But what if the factual element wasn't important? What if the book didn't even exist? Do you need Ten Commandments to guide your ethics? Or do you just need to know what feels right in your heart? Do unto others, as you would have them do unto you. That is a basic principle that sums up the entire life premise in regards to treating people with kindness.

At some point, we all need to do our own intervention and look at our actions. In order to progress as a human, it has nothing to do with posting scriptures or making people feel as though they are lesser. It's about choosing love, affecting lives positively, and putting in the noble work beyond Sunday service.

．．．．．

Week 24 To-Do List: Do you have any words from a book, a scripture, a sermon, a phrase, a motto, or a quote that you use to guide your moves? I have quotes hanging up in my office for students to read, but sometimes I sit and read all of them and interpret the meaning and try to figure out the reason they might have been created. I notice which ones speak to the youth and which ones speak to adults. If you don't have any words that inspire you, find a quote, psalm, or phrase and print it out somewhere so you can see it daily. Use it when necessary.

WEEK 25

THE WAY WE PRAY

I don't want to judge you, so I hope that's it's ok,
If I ask about your faith and how you move from day to day?
Do the thoughts you think, deeds you do, and words that you say,
Align with being divine and how do you pray?
Do you close your eyes and bow your head and clasp your hands requesting,
For better health, to bless your food, for love, or job progression?
Are you running down a list of desires, money, possessions?
Do you say Hail Marys when you sin? Are you confessing?
Is it five times a day that you get down on both knees?
Do you remember the gift of life, when someone close to you leaves, and you grieve?
When you're not inside of a church,
Are you only mentioning God when you hear someone sneeze?
So let's forget the "How," the better question is "When,"
At night before bed? Or when you need some pain to end?
With the team before the game?
With the crew before the show?
With your fam before a flight?
At a wake when someone goes?
I know it sounds like I'm getting in your business, maybe so,
But I don't need an answer, I need you to know,
Do you only pray for health when you're sick?
Money when you're struggling?
Nourishment when you're starving?
Sanity when you're bugging?
Employment when you're jobless?
Stability when it's gone?
Are you praying for companionship only when you're alone?

If that's the case, I want to challenge you today,
To switch up how you do it, and try it a different way,
No matter how much you make, be grateful for your pay,
If you sleep inside of a home, give thanks for where you stay,
If there's food in your fridge, or on your table, say grace,
If your body's feeling great, be glad you're awake,
If you're happily married, or single and having dates,
The most amazing date is today's date,
So whether your eyes are open or closed,
Palms up or hands together,
The deity, the place or the method, it's whatever,
When you're weathering a storm,
You pray to God to make it better,
But when life is bright and sunny,
Do you forget Her?
When do you pray?

Lenny S. captured this photo of me outside of a mosque in Morocco in 2005.
It was such a beautiful vision. I was thirsty for knowledge.

THE WAY WE PRAY

I don't want to judge you, so I hope that's it's ok,
If I ask about your faith and how you move from day to day?
Do the thoughts you think, deeds you do, and words that you say,
Align with being divine and how do you pray?

Although I started this verse with a disclaimer, you may feel judged anyway after reading this. In my defense, I want to enhance your approach to your faith and I started writing this facing the mirror. I've always wondered since I was young and I was taught to get down on my knees, close my eyes, speak to God, and ask for stuff, if I was really getting anywhere with that course of action.

I didn't like prayer to resemble a verbal Christmas list for Santa Claus, so it was important that I was always thankful when I prayed, and I felt weird blatantly asking for specific things.

Do you close your eyes and bow your head and clasp your hands requesting,
For better health, to bless your food, for love or job progression?
Are you running down a list of desires, money, possessions?
Do you say Hail Marys when you sin? Are you confessing?
Is it five times a day that you get down on both knees?
Do you remember the gift of life, when someone close to you leaves, and you grieve?
When you're not inside of a church,
Are you only mentioning God, when you hear someone sneeze?

When I was composing this section, I wanted to touch on different religious practices used in Christianity, Islam, and Catholicism. Everyone prays differently and maybe reading these words will help you realize that prayer doesn't need to be one way. Perhaps the rigid idea of religion often restricts followers when we all should act as leaders. This is not to suggest that you should not carry out religious habits or claim a denomination. But it is to suggest that we should all strive to live a life that is exemplary of the teachings and paths walked by the sacred and saintly. That means that it is more important to walk like Christ than to put a title on your religious faction.

So let's forget the "How," the better question is "When,"
At night before bed? Or when you need some pain to end?
With the team before the game?
With the crew before the show?
With your fam before a flight?
At a wake, when someone goes?
I know it sounds like I'm getting in your business, maybe so,
But I don't need an answer, I need you to know,

As we go below the surface and unearth the act of prayer, I want to look at the reason most of us begin to speak to The Creator. What sparks the conversation that happens between you and the higher power? Is it a daily routine before meals and sleep? Is it at the time of need when you post on a social media wall asking others to deliver their own words of prayer?

I had to internalize the reason and time that I pray the most. I discovered that I used to pray during times of need but now my prayers take place in the mornings when I wake up and at times where I feel God's favor throughout my day. At one point I believed it was wrong to pray for worldly possessions and minor miracles. Now I understand that it is perfectly fine to welcome abundance whether it's financial abundance, wellness, or good fortune. There is no rule that says that you can't expect and accept wonderful experiences, the key is to wholeheartedly appreciate the blessings if they are immense or tiny.

Do you only pray for health when you're sick?
Money when you're struggling?
Nourishment when you're starving?
Sanity when you're bugging?
Employment when you're jobless?
Stability when it's gone?
Are you praying for companionship only when you're alone?

If this is you, don't be defensive or offended. It is human nature to call upon a supernatural force to assist you when it feels like you're out of earthly options for relief. Is God listening to you? Are your prayers really just acts of habit that bring peace to your heart? What if the secret to prayer, like all things, is to humbly be gracious and grateful for what you have? Then prayer would not only come at a time when there is stress, strife, or hardship. You would pray without a request. You would pray because your eyes can see. You would pray because you can walk. You would pray because you are alive and well.

If that's the case, I want to challenge you today,
To switch up how you do it, and try it a different way,
No matter how much you make, be grateful for your pay,
If you sleep inside of a home, give thanks for where you stay,
If there's food in your fridge, or on your table, say grace,
If your body's feeling great, be glad you're awake,
If you're happily married, or single and having dates,
The most amazing date is today's date,
So whether your eyes are open or closed,
Palms up or hands together,
The deity, the place or the method, it's whatever,
When you're weathering a storm,
You pray to God to make it better,
But when life is bright and sunny,
Do you forget Her?
When do you pray?

It really doesn't matter how you pray or when. What matters is your overall gratitude for every experience. Praying is just an acknowledgment.

I used to play on a basketball team with two brothers whom I greatly admired, Slim and Abdul, and they were Muslim. Sometimes our games would fall at a time in the evening when they needed to pray. There was one particular game where our team had only five players, with Slim and Abdul being a part of that five. The brothers were present during warm-ups but before the game started, they went to a separate area of the gym to pray. The game was about to start. There were eight players and two referees on the court, standing around. The other team was a bit confused. My team knew Slim and Abdul were praying and we let the others know. Although they were unsure how long the delay would be, they were respectful and understanding. After three minutes of patient waiting, the two brothers trotted onto the court, apologizing for the delay. The reaction from every person on that court was consistent: There was nothing more important than the two brothers' faith at that moment, and none of us needed an apology.

That experience made me think about the act of prayer in the middle of a hectic day. I thought about how comfortable that must have felt to kneel next to your brother and give thanks and praise to your deity, no matter what was happening around them. I love that about Islam. That experience on the court caused me to drop the rules when it comes to prayer. I don't need to close my eyes, kneel, or hold my hands in a certain way all the time, but then sometimes I do. Sometimes in order to block out the world, my body needs to be in tune with my thoughts. And more often I pray when things are going well. I am grateful when I'm healthy, when I can pay bills, when I eat a meal, when my sons wake up, when my wife smiles at me. Don't wait.

· · · · ·

Week 25 To-Do List: Pray every day this week. You don't need to do anything physically, you don't need to speak out loud, and you don't have to ask for one thing. All I'm asking you to do is stop and acknowledge the love in your life and give thanks as you attract more of that energy into your experience.

WEEK 26

THE 2020 HINDSIGHT (WHAT MATTERS MOST)

During these times we feel lost, anxious, we're finding ways to cope,
There's sadness mixed with gratitude,
Fear bundled with hope,
We feel optimistic but realistic, keeping loved ones close,
While the rest are in our prayers, we're reminded what matters most,
It's not the dumb argument that made you stop communication,
With somebody that you love, although they caused some huge frustration,
It's not the irking friend that had you vexed and losing patience,
Or the relative that's negative,
There's doctors losing patients,
And healthcare workers and first responders are riding,
To keep people from dying, and telling us stay inside,
And a lot of us are complying, but this is a new precedent,
Wonder would this happen if we had a new president,
Folks are sick and nervous that they might just leave the earth,
And they can't even get a hug, and if they pass, we can't have service,
Now's the time to put your pride aside, and go beneath the surface,
You studied those Bible verses, now show love to every person
Call your family, call acquaintances, friends, even your foes,
The world is cold but if your heart isn't <u>frozen</u>, <u>let it go</u>,
We are all God's children and only God knows,
How this thing is going to end so once again, I must impose,
With honest words, talking bars, thought-food nourishment,
Not telling you how to live, this is encouragement,
To ask yourself what matters,   .
The money you were worshipping?
The home that you're furnishing?
The food that you're purchasing?

The kids that are flourishing?
The job that you're servicing?
You used to want to work from home,
Now you're home working,
And you feel like a kid upset at his homework,
You like apocalyptic movies, we're living our own version,
So while you're watching live posts,
And more humans become ghosts,
And you worry about your gross income becoming gross,
Be thankful for the time you've been allotted,
It's a lot, but it's giving you a chance to ask yourself,
What matters most?

L to R. Daddy, Zaire, Cairo, and Mommy on a 2020 trip to the aquarium. Masks required.

THE 2020 HINDSIGHT (WHAT MATTERS MOST)

During these times we feel lost, anxious, we're finding ways to cope,
There's sadness mixed with gratitude,
Fear bundled with hope,
We feel optimistic, but realistic, keeping loved ones close,
While the rest are in our prayers, we're reminded what matters most,

This piece was composed during 2020. I included this because the world is currently enduring a period of indecision, worry, and confusion, and for most of us, we feel afraid. As the pandemic spreads and folks are forced to stay home, these days are also marked by racial tension due to the recorded murder of George Floyd by the hands of the Minneapolis Police Department and the Jacob Blake shooting in Wisconsin. The killings became the spark for protests, rallies, more violence, and an unprecedented awakening by many humans of all backgrounds.

The call for action is prevalent in society; popular companies, organizations, and anyone that agrees that all people should be treated equally are choosing to speak up. More importantly, there is a heightened awareness of the truth behind the targeting of African-Americans in society specifically by law enforcement. A horrific disease has brought about several waves of uncharted emotional territory that has forced us all to reconsider what we truly value. I had to include this verse as a part of this peculiar capsule of time.

It's not the dumb argument that made you stop communication,
With somebody that you love, although they caused some huge frustration,
It's not the irking friend that had you vexed and losing patience,
Or the relative that's negative, there's doctors losing patients,
And healthcare workers and first responders are riding,
To keep people from dying, and telling us stay inside,

Over the years, I can remember having unofficial rifts with friends and family members that turned into weeks or months of zero contact with each other.

In some of those instances, I was the "bigger person" that reached out to find some kind of resolve for a misunderstanding. In other cases, I was firm in my position that some people can be loved from afar. When the Coronavirus struck the world, many people lost their lives. And while we should always value our friendships and loved ones, being forced to stay away from everyone outside of your home creates a larger desire for personal contact.

There are still friendships that I haven't mended because I feel like I am not at fault. I'm sure you can empathize with that stance even though I am encouraging myself to change and accept that a loved one can be a lost one at any moment. I have so many friends in the healthcare field and the fear of the unknown grows daily as I write this. What I can hope for is that by the time you read this, there is some normalcy restored to the world, but either way, things will never be the same.

And a lot of us are complying, but this is a new precedent,
Wonder would this happen if we had a new president,
Folks are sick and nervous that they might just leave the earth,
And they can't even get a hug, and if they pass, we can't have service,
Now's the time to put your pride aside, and go beneath the surface,
You studied those Bible verses; now show love to every person
Call your family, call acquaintances, friends, even your foes,
The world is cold but if your heart isn't <u>frozen</u>, <u>let it go</u>,
We are all God's children and only God knows,
How this thing is going to end so once again, I must impose,
With honest words, talking bars, thought-food nourishment,
Not telling you how to live, this is encouragement,

Of course when a crisis occurs, there is always some mention of the cause and talk of prevention. We may never truthfully know the reason for this outbreak and we can only speculate that there should have been a plan in place for prevention and to halt the spread. What we can control is how we move going forward.

I referenced the Holy Book once again only to make a point that the mission and reason for filling your soul with good intentions and knowledge of psalms and proverbs to implement the words through actions. Even while I preach enlightenment, I don't always practice uplifting others. When we were first under quarantine orders in March of 2020, I made it my business to make random phone calls and send text messages to people that I did not speak to regularly. But as time passed, I became wrapped up in my own family life. Like so many others, I yearned for the basic pleasures of the outside world. So while I am still finding peace in my heart to reach out to more individuals I was once close to, I am also searching my soul at the end of every day to find highlights that keep me smiling. Even though the year 2020 looks nothing like I envisioned it would, there is always room for gratitude.

To ask yourself what matters,
The money you were worshipping?
The home that you're furnishing?
The food that you're purchasing?
The kids that are flourishing?
The job that you're servicing?
You used to want to work from home,
Now you're home working,
And you feel like a kid upset at his homework,

Currently, my wife and I are fortunate enough to earn from home. Even though having our two young boys in the house with us can make us slightly stir-crazy, it is a blessing.

There was a particular day that my wife and I had multiple meetings in succession, my oldest son was incredibly needy, and wanted to do math and vowel lessons while the baby was cranky and clingy. I was hungry, tired, annoyed with being stuck inside, and I was bothered that both of us had to work instead of just focusing on our children.

And then I thought about a typical work day where we would have had to wake up at a certain time and get ourselves and the boys dressed, put together lunch, drive them to school, and drive to work. I would have to interact with students and co-workers, dive deep into other people's problems, feel sleepy at times, find time to eat a rushed lunch, miss my family, have to drive again to pick the boys up, figure out dinner, put them to bed, prepare for the next day, and try to squeeze in quality time with my wife for a couple of hours before we were both too exhausted to do much of anything.

It hit me at that moment that the reality of going to work every day was a blessing that caused me to desire more time at home. And now that I'm home, the Universe is giving me a chance to appreciate these moments before things are somewhat back to the way they were. It's okay to be irked by a current situation, but find a way to make peace with every setting that you are placed in and the joy will fill you up from the inside out.

You like apocalyptic movies, we're living our own version,
So while you're watching live posts,
And more humans become ghosts,
And you worry about your gross income becoming gross,
Be thankful for the time you've been allotted,
It's a lot, but it's giving you a chance to ask yourself,
What matters most?

Whether it's *Birdbox*, *Contagion*, *I Am Legend*, or *Pandemic*, people love to watch an engaging story that deals with the possible end of the world at the hands of something man made. Most of us watch and wonder what we would do in a similar situation to the film we're watching. Life often imitates art and in this moment, our lives are being altered in a brand new way that creates an upheaval of truth and terror in many cases. The terror lies in the hearts of Americans that do not know if a trip to the supermarket or a package from the postal service could be the conduit for hospitalization and quarantine. At the same time, bigots and racists are using their voices to express their contempt for other groups of people.

The understanding of the African descendant plight in the USA is gaining national attention as more and more Caucasians are expressing their newfound identification of their own privilege, and the systemic, strategic plot to cage, mentally confine, and exterminate people of color by any means necessary. What can you do with this information? If by the time you're experiencing these words, you've lived through the laborious year of 2020, I pray there is light illuminating every step of your travels. At this time, we have the option to appreciate the positive moments from this dreaded stitch in the infinite timeline. The moments contain time to yourself, working in the comfort of your home, being closer to loved ones, saving money that would otherwise be used on outings and gas, and the highest on my list of pluses, is identifying what matters most.

Basketball, vacationing with the family, eating at restaurants, having multiple friends over, and physical salutations from hugs to handshakes are all valid slices of life that contributed to my happiness that I miss. I have barely done any of these things I just mentioned in order to preserve the health of my family. My immediate family matters most to me. My mother and my family in Florida matter the most to me. My brother and his family matter the most to me. When my wife and I wake up healthy, and my two boys are active and well, it is the daily goal and true triumph that is unmatched. Although this may not be the ideal circumstance to elevate your God-level conscious meter, and you may not believe every gem I've handed you since you started reading, please consider this if nothing else, joy is within, gratitude starts with small words of thanks and expands to include who and whatever you want to be appreciative of. Remember that love is limitless.

· · · · ·

Week 26 To-Do List: The Coronavirus has brought about inconvenience, prohibited you from a normal vacation, outings, decreased ease and comfort when in the close proximity of friends, and kept you and the ones you love indoors for a lofty part of the year. With that in mind, I want you to write down every beautiful aspect of life that has been highlighted by the effects of this awful malady. List all the things that made you feel fortunate whether it's staying home from work, or less traffic on the roads, more time with immediate fam, or saving money. I would like to salute every healthcare worker that sacrifices their time and risks infection to help others. Compile the list and review it once you're done. Within the words you've written, you have most likely identified the core of your essence and you've realized what matters most.

\